THE CHANGING HR FUNCTION:

Transforming HR?

Peter Reilly

Penny Tamkin

Andrea Broughton

The Chartered Institute of Personnel and Development is the leading publisher of books
and reports for personnel and training professionals, students, and all those concerned
with the effective management and development of people at work.
For full details of all our titles, please contact the Publishing Department:
Tel: 020 8612 6204
E-mail: publish@cipd.co.uk

To view and purchase all CIPD titles:
www.cipd.co.uk/bookstore

For details of CIPD research projects:
www.cipd.co.uk/research

THE CHANGING HR FUNCTION:

Transforming HR?

Peter Reilly
Penny Tamkin
Andrea Broughton
INSTITUTE FOR EMPLOYMENT STUDIES

First published 2007

Cover and text design by Sutchinda Rangsi-Thompson
Typeset by Paperweight
Printed in Great Britain by Short Run Press, Exeter

British Library Cataloguing in Publication Data
A catalogue record for this book is available from the British Library

ISBN-13   978 1 84398 197 8

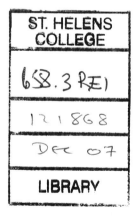

Chartered Institute of Personnel and Development,
151 The Broadway, London SW19 1JQ

Tel: 020 8612 6200
Website: www.cipd.co.uk

Incorporated by Royal Charter. Registered charity no. 1079797.

CONTENTS

ACKNOWLEDGEMENTS

The CIPD would like to thank Peter Reilly from the Institute of Employment Studies (IES) who undertook this research. Thanks also to all of the individuals who took time to complete the survey which forms a key part of the research. Finally, we would like to extend our thanks to the following organisations for contributing to this research:

- Cable and Wireless

- Ernst and Young (UK) *

- Capita *

- Firefly Communications *

- Hampshire County Council *

- Surrey County Council *

- Her Majesty's Revenue and Customs *

- Nortel *

- Vodafone *

- Reuters

- The Ministry of Defence

- Fujitsu Services

- E.ON

(*Further details of the HR structures of these organisations are to be found in Appendix 2.)

FOREWORD

We have highlighted the HR function as a key area for research for numerous reasons. We believe that it is intrinsically interesting for most of our members at a time when major challenges are facing HR functions and when the majority of larger ones are being reorganised and roles changed in response. In light of this, the CIPD wanted to be able to provide a clear position in terms of how to best organise/skill the HR function to succeed in the future.

Since the project began two years ago, the CIPD has already published various reports:

❖ *The HR Function: Today's challenges; tomorrow's direction* (CIPD Report, 2006)

❖ *The Changing HR Function: The key questions* (Change Agenda, 2006)

❖ *The Changing HR Function* (Survey report, September, 2007)

This Research Report has been produced by the CIPD as the fourth and final comprehensive output of a two-year research project into the changing HR function, drawing in particular on the results of a survey and detailed interviews within a number of organisations. It aims to provide practical guidance for organisations on how best to structure and staff their HR function.

We are very interested in your thoughts on this research, so if you have any comments, please let us know.

Vanessa Robinson
Manager, Organisation and Resourcing

EXECUTIVE SUMMARY

This Research Report aims to describe the evolution and current state of the HR function and to provide practical guidance for organisations on how best to structure and staff the function to achieve future success. It is the final stage of a larger project within the CIPD's research programme on the HR function, and its particular focus is on the impact of HR transformation. This research stage has used case studies and a quantitative survey to examine how HR functions are meeting the challenges of changes to structure, roles, skills and relationships. Comparisons have also been made with the CIPD's 2003 research: *HR Survey: Where we are, where we are heading*.

A number of key messages emerged from the research. Firstly, it appeared that HR's main contribution comes from two sources: its service delivery and facilitation roles. The former encompasses the recruitment and retention of staff and ensures that they have the requisite competencies to do their work. The facilitation role of HR is perhaps less clearly defined, but it concerns encouraging/coaching managers to get the most from their staff. Both these inputs can be at the operational and strategic levels. How these roles are balanced depends upon the business objectives and the way they relate to people.

Moreover, some organisations believed that HR has a governance role to play in order to protect organisational values. While it is clear from the research that HR might not champion employees, or normally deal with individual cases, many organisations are interested in the collective performance of employees through employee engagement, corporate social responsibility (CSR) and employer branding – although HR would seem to be more active in the former two than the latter. Nevertheless, some HR managers worried that the function was becoming too distant from employees, and, indeed, some case study organisations had taken steps to find ways of being more approachable.

A second finding was that the three-legged stool model (shared services, centres of expertise and business partners), attributed to Dave Ulrich, was the most common HR function structure, although fewer than 30% of our survey respondents said that they had introduced the model in full and an equal proportion had only partly introduced it. As to the legs of the stool, the use of business partners is much more common than either shared service centres or centres of expertise.

Where such a model had not been introduced, the most common type of structure was a single HR team incorporating generalists, specialists and administration. Although some contributors worried that HR is tending to 'follow the Ulrich fashion', these figures suggest that this concern is overstated. Yet there were also worries that HR's change programme is disconnected, both from the business strategy and any other structural modernisation taking place elsewhere in the organisation. This concern is compounded by questions over whether HR is setting its change objectives clearly enough and sufficiently engaging managers, executives and the HR community effectively in change design and execution.

This point is perhaps reinforced by the fact that the primary driver for structural transformation is the desire for the HR function to be a more strategic contributor. This came out top in the survey – above the need to improve service standards, to increase business focus or even to reduce costs. In fact, according to the survey, the HR function has doubled the proportion of time it spent on strategic inputs over the last three years, at the expense of administrative activities. Whether structural change is the cause of this shift is less clear. However, although developing HR strategy and policy and contributing to business strategy were the most important tasks for survey respondents, providing support for line managers and HR administration were still their most time-consuming tasks, suggesting that further progress in rebalancing the workload is indeed necessary.

Looking at the components of the three-legged stool structure, from our case study organisations we found a great deal of variation in the formats used. There were different conceptions of the business partner role: business partnering may involve, to varying extents, operational delivery to and support for the line; business partners may be solo operators or part of a team; and business partners might report to HR or to the business unit head. Moreover, although there was a positive appreciation of the work of business partners, there were a number of challenges faced regarding their role and relationships with others.

We found, as expected, that shared services is a phenomenon for large – rather than small – organisations. Overall, the structure of shared services varies by organisation, especially in a global context. Only 4% of our survey respondents said that they wholly outsourced their HR shared services operation, and around a quarter outsourced part of their shared services activities. We came across other examples where HR shared services had been transferred out of the function but not out of the organisation, and we found cross-functional as well as single HR service centres.

Outsourcing therefore remains a tactical rather than a strategic matter for most organisations, limited in scope mainly to specific activities where specialist skills are not available. The exception was where outsourcing was considered to fund technological investment.

Our survey results indicate that nearly two thirds of those organisations that have introduced shared services have also created centres of expertise. Learning and development was the commonest centre of expertise, followed by recruitment, reward and employee relations. In some organisations, expertise is held within the business unit, so that it aligns with specific unit needs, or performed corporately, rather than in separate subject-based units.

Problems associated with the introduction of the three-legged stool model particularly relate to include the difficulties posed by segmented service provision. So gaps in service provision, boundary management and communication were the principal problem areas, according to the survey. Role definitions in practice, rather than theory, and skill (or resource) shortages were also cited as key challenges. Filling cracks in the system – especially to provide operational support for line managers – was identified as the most likely effective solution.

The overall impression from the survey was that structural change had little impact on development upwards or sideways, or in joining the function. Two thirds of our survey respondents said that the changes gave more opportunity to staff compared with only 17% who thought that it was harder to develop people into new roles. There were different views

expressed by more junior members of the HR community. They were apparently more concerned than managers about the implications of new organisational structures on career development.

Besides structural change, process modernisation was a priority in many organisations, not least because the quality of HR processes was perceived as its weakest area by CEOs, in the view of HR managers. Technology was frequently a key enabler of reform, although securing the necessary financial investment was not always easy, even where there were demonstrable savings, and successful implementation was a challenge for a third of the survey respondents. There was debate about whether process change should precede or follow structural change, and where systems investment sits in the sequence. No clear picture emerged from our research as to best practice, because much depended on the organisational starting point and characteristics. Process automation had brought real benefits, but we found that care was needed with self-service to avoid managers feeling 'dumped on'. Standardisation of processes was an important driver for change (especially in global organisations) and brought benefits in terms of simplification, use of good practice and benchmarking, but concerns were expressed that, if extended into the policy arena, a single approach to a varied work environment might be imposed.

Looking at the relationships of the HR function with managers, we found that the division of people management responsibilities between HR and the line was largely unchanged since 2003, despite HR's wish to have more work transferred to line managers. HR still takes the lead on remuneration and implementing redundancies; the line has prime responsibility for work organisation; whereas for recruitment, employee relations and training and development activity is more shared. Overall, the principal reasons for HR's lack of success in achieving greater transfer of tasks to the line appear to be line manager priorities, their skills, the time available to them for people management tasks and poor manager self-service.

On measurement, it was noteworthy that HR appeared not just to be assessing its process performance but also considering its broader effectiveness. Thus, virtually all organisations measured HR's efficiency, and over half examined HR effectiveness through people management practice and its effect on outcomes such as absence. The main indicators used were business performance, surveys of managers/employees and customer satisfaction metrics. System or policy evaluation still did not appear to be particularly common, which is problematic when considering the success of HR transformation.

We found that there has not been a great deal of change in terms of the skills needs of the function since 2003. In general, senior HR managers seemed more concerned with the skills required of the business partners – such as political and

influencing skills – than the general (interpersonal) skills
required of the function.

Finally, where development takes place, the emphasis appears
to be more on formal training than on experiential learning.
Moreover, there was not a great deal of evidence in the survey
of a policy of challenging staff or encouraging learning through
measures such as short-term assignments, project work and
covering absence.

INTRODUCTION

❖ **The Introduction outlines the relationship of this Report to previous and ongoing research.**

❖ **It also outlines the structure of this Report.**

This report is the final stage of a larger project within the CIPD's research programme on the HR function. It aims to describe the evolution and current state of the function and to provide practical guidance for organisations on how best to structure and staff the function to achieve future success. The particular focus of this project is the impact of HR transformation on the structure, processes and staffing of organisations. Previous CIPD research has looked at technology, relationships with managers, HR careers and HR's role in change. These results are drawn upon as relevant, but this particular report starts with the fact that there is a dearth of information on structural change. A number of organisations have implemented the so-called Ulrich model (a structure with business partners, centres of expertise and shared services), but how many organisations have gone down this route and what has been their experience thus far is not known.

The first stage of this project aimed to review present knowledge and identify research themes for the subsequent phases. It did this through a literature review and discussions with leading practitioners and academics. Discussions explored the current and future challenges for the function, in particular views on the 'new' HR operating model, the move to transfer HR activity to line management, experiences of e-HR, measuring the function's performance and the resourcing of the function, including the development of skills and careers. The results of this work were published in autumn 2006 as *The Changing HR Function: The key questions*.

The second and third phases of the project have involved original research through case studies and a survey to examine how HR functions across the spectrums of size and sector are meeting the challenges of structure, roles, skills and relationships. The aim has thus been to explore further the same territory as the first phase of the research but through

more in-depth discussions with organisations and through a quantitative survey.

THE SURVEY

The questions used in this survey drew upon the questionnaire used for the CIPD's 2003 survey of the HR function (CIPD, 2003), the 2006 report for the first stage of this project and the case-study findings of the second stage.

Two formats were used – paper and online – for respondents' convenience. The CIPD contacted the most senior HR job-holder in UK organisations on their database, and sent out 12,000 invitations to complete the survey (2,000 were sent via email and 10,000 by post). A total of 787 responses were collected by the deadline of April 2007, two thirds of which had been provided on paper and one third through the online questionnaire. Around 84% of the respondents were CIPD members. As to level in the organisation, 88% were heads of HR or board members. Just over a third worked for multinational organisations.

Of the survey response by sector, 20% was from manufacturing/production, 40% from private sector services, and the bulk of the rest from the public sector. By size, nearly half of the responses came from organisations with over 1,000 employees, whereas at the other end of the spectrum, a quarter employed 250 or fewer staff.

The full survey results are published in a separate report, *The Changing HR Function, Survey Report*, September 2007, but the simple frequency of responses to the questions is set out in Appendix 1.

THE CASE STUDIES

Our discussions with organisations were many and various. In some organisations we spoke to leading members of the HR function, conducted focus groups with less senior staff and interviewed line managers. In other organisations we spoke only to HR staff – usually those involved in an HR transformation project.

We used a structured discussion guide to capture information on HR's purpose, the contents of its work, its structure, roles and processes, work sourcing, relationships with stakeholders, measurement of functional performance, careers, skills and future challenges. Not all the questions were asked of all the organisations. Discussion focused on the key questions that applied to that organisation.

Another input to the research was a discussion group convened by the CIPD in Dublin with senior HR professionals. This was similar to the debate, hosted by RBS, which contributed to the findings of this project at Stage 1 (reported in *The HR Function: Today's challenges, tomorrow's direction*, Event Report, CIPD, May 2006).

THIS REPORT

This Research Report is deliberately structured to follow the approach of *The Changing HR Function: The key questions*. There is an introduction to each chapter that briefly summarises the previous report. The research findings of this stage of the project are then presented, combining the survey and case study material. Comparisons are made with the CIPD's 2003 research, where appropriate. A more discursive examination of the implications of the evidence described follows, drawing on evidence from other CIPD research and determining whether the results presented here support or refute earlier evidence. There are then learning points for practitioners at the end of each chapter.

> **'The report begins with the purpose of the HR function before moving on...to cover structures, processes, outsourcing, specific new roles, relationships with managers, measurement of the HR function and skills and development.'**

The report begins with the purpose of the HR function before moving on in successive chapters to cover structures, processes, outsourcing, specific new roles, relationships with managers, measurement of the HR function and skills and development. One chapter has been added to the previous format – managing HR transformation – because this seemed to be relevant to the interest of many practitioners.

There are two appendices. The first contains the results from the survey; the second summarises the main case studies in terms of their organisational characteristics and HR structure.

THE PURPOSE OF HR

2

❖ **From the survey, two principal tasks emerged: HR as a deliverer of services and HR as facilitator of the line's people management role.**

❖ **In addition, some organisations are clear that HR has a governance role to protect organisational values.**

❖ **HR might not champion employees nor normally deal with individual cases, but many organisations are actively pursuing employee engagement.**

❖ **A number of definitions of how HR adds value were proposed. How they apply relates to the organisation's business model.**

INTRODUCTION

The purpose of the HR function has been much debated, perhaps overly so. In an earlier CIPD report (*The Changing HR Function: The key questions*), we explored a range of ideas in relation to the role of HR. Many organisations have been concerned to increase the value HR offers its business customers and to enable HR to become more strategic and business-focused. They have tried to achieve this by using a variety of means, especially through structural change, e-HR, outsourcing non-core activities, the standardisation of policies and processes, and the devolution of people management responsibilities to the line. The aim of these developments has been to shift HR from playing the 'clerk of the works' role to one in which it is perceived as a 'strategic architect' (Tyson and Fell, 1986).

Another point of debate has been to what extent HR should fulfil, and is fulfilling, all four of the quadrants in Ulrich's 1997

description of the role of HR (see Figure 1): strategic partner, change agent, employee champion, and administrative expert (Ulrich, 1997).

In particular, there has been discussion of what the employee champion's role might be and whether HR should be discharging it.

A final aspect of doubt about HR's role concerns its content. Debate has been concerned with whether learning and development is an integral part of HR, and similarly OD. How important corporate social responsibility (CSR) and employer branding are to the work of the function is another recent question raised. And whether employee well-being is a revitalised area for HR's consideration is a further matter considered.

There is also a fundamental question over the role HR plays with respect to the organisation as a whole and to its managers. Is HR a support function, is it an advisory one, or does it have more of a regulatory role?

RESEARCH RESULTS

Introduction

We asked our case-study organisations and our survey respondents about what HR exists to do. Responses varied. For some HR was there to provide operational support and to create a policy and practice infrastructure. Others stressed the role of HR as the leader of people management, with engagement highlighted as a key tool by some. Another group took a more prosaic perspective of the same goal, seeing HR as there to 'raise performance'. Lower on the list in the survey –

Figure 1 ❖ Ulrich's model of HR's roles	
Strategic partner	Change agent
Employee champion	Administrative expert

Source: Ulrich (1997)

THE PURPOSE OF HR

3

Figure 2 ✦ **Main objectives of the HR function (top five priorities)**

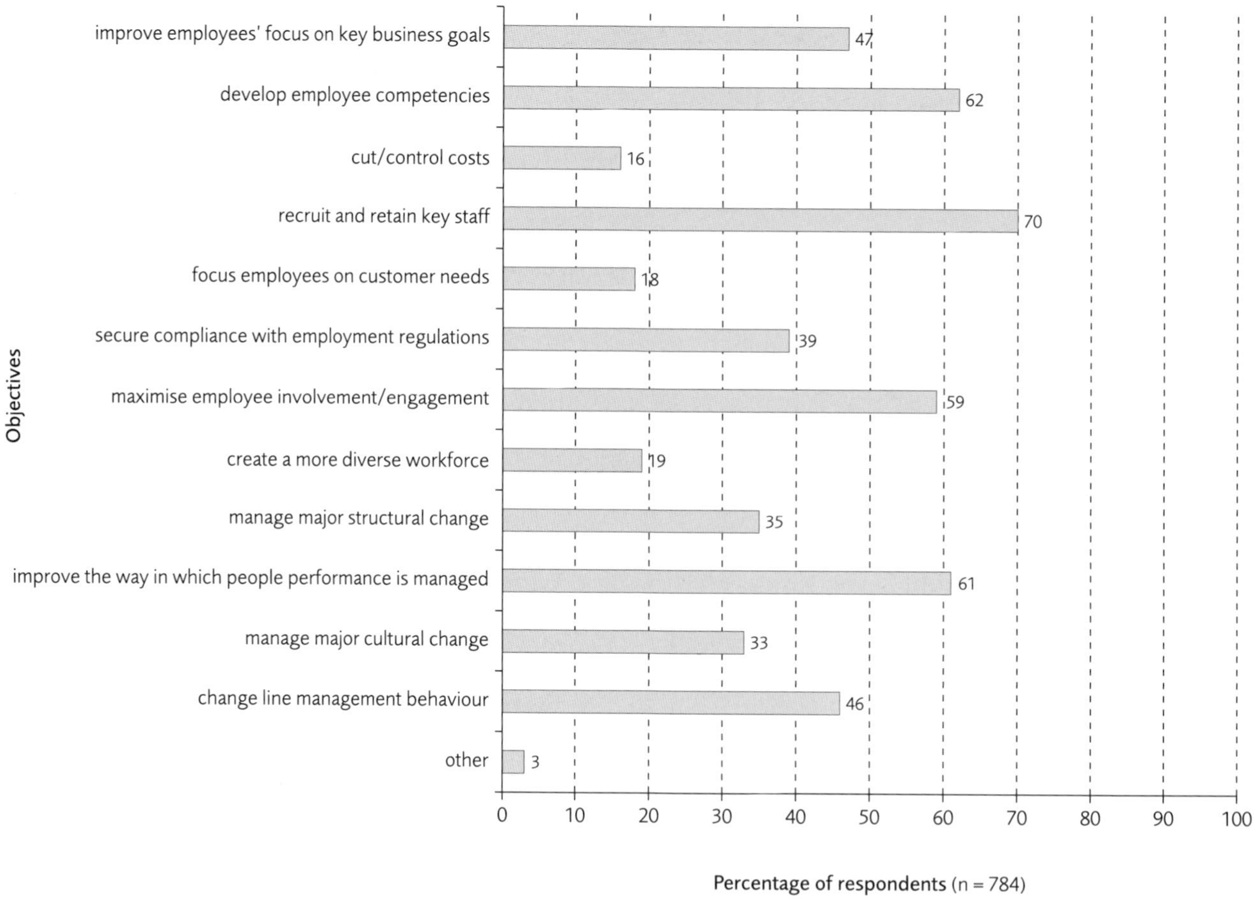

Objective	Percentage
improve employees' focus on key business goals	47
develop employee competencies	62
cut/control costs	16
recruit and retain key staff	70
focus employees on customer needs	18
secure compliance with employment regulations	39
maximise employee involvement/engagement	59
create a more diverse workforce	19
manage major structural change	35
improve the way in which people performance is managed	61
manage major cultural change	33
change line management behaviour	46
other	3

Percentage of respondents (n = 784)

Source: CIPD survey (2007)

but more important in the case studies – was HR's role in cost reduction or increased employee efficiency.

The issue of HR's regulatory or governance role and the narrower issue of compliance with employment regulations were also issues debated by case-study participants.

These topics are examined in more detail below, but Figure 2 sets out the responses to a survey question on HR's main objectives. This shows that recruitment and retention is the highest-priority item on the list, followed by developing competencies and maximising employee involvement and engagement. These were all leading issues in the 2003 survey.

Service deliverer

In these survey results a key theme that emerged was HR's role as a deliverer of services (recruitment and retention, competence development). As a service deliverer HR contributes by helping to get the right people in the right place at the right time and to develop their skills. It offers expertise and appropriate policies. This, in some eyes, is to be combined

with providing a policy and systems infrastructure within which line managers operate.

This sort of role is perhaps put into words by a Divisional Director at Capita:

The role of HR is to offer advice and guidance – from the setting of overall people policy to advice and guidance on the ground and the interpretation of that policy. HR has a leading role in the organisation with regard to people policies and practices, but then hands over to the business. HR has a large role in creating corporate identity and the framework for people management. They are not policemen, but will point out if decisions don't fit with the culture and will highlight HR implications. They assist when things go wrong, and can help avoid employment tribunals. Increasingly, with the raft of employment legislation, management requires HR people to spend more time getting to grips with the legal situation and supporting the line in this context. They assist with absence management and give advice on pay awards. HR is not an 'employee champion'. They don't act on individual cases, which is the line managers' responsibility.

The message here is on setting the framework within which people are managed and advising managers as appropriate. As the respondent said in the interview, this is the sort of role HR has played for some time – strong on operational support and policy infrastructure.

In some situations, HR moves from a more operational role in service delivery to a more strategic role. Thus at Capita, HR gets involved in both operational issues (such as absence and turnover) and specific business issues to do with potential new business (the function may contribute in the sales process). Its work on TUPE transfers/acquisitions can be both practical and of strategic importance. Similarly, at Fujitsu Services – a company that manages outsourced IT services – HR's support to the company's outsourcing bidding process may be a commercial differentiator through the way in which it can transfer and integrate staff in an effective manner.

Facilitator of line management

A second role that was apparent from survey responses on the main objectives of HR was to facilitate the line's people management responsibility. Getting the most out of people does not necessarily mean HR taking a hands-on position. The line manager is primarily responsible for getting the most out of staff. HR, as a facilitator, aims to maximise the people contribution through helping managers do the managing.

The context of this role may vary. In some cases, facilitation was, as we will see below, about improving the performance of the organisation through people. In other circumstances the focus was on coaching the line to perform their people management tasks better. A third element was HR's contributing to change management by offering solutions to managers to move the organisation forward.

Strategic people focus

The challenge of HR transformation in many organisations is to deepen the contribution to organisational success and add value at the strategic level. This can be realised by releasing the energies of the workforce. Some survey respondents wanted to emphasise HR's leadership role on people management. For example, one survey respondent wrote that HR's purpose is 'to provide the business with strategic leadership in the provision of people-centric programmes'. Another survey respondent said that the purpose of HR was to 'create value through people'; while a third wrote that HR was there 'to extract maximum value from our human resource'. This is very much an active rather than a passive operation and was also a theme in a number of our case studies.

As for how HR could create this strategic people focus, some of our case-study participants, including line managers, saw one of HR's strengths as being the overview it had of people management across the organisation and the contribution it could make to developing a corporate identity. This was related to HR's role in facilitating cultural change, where that identity might be being adjusted.

> **'HR's purpose is "to provide the business with strategic leadership in the provision of people-centric programmes"..."[to] create value through people"..."to extract maximum value from our human resource".'**

More specifically, there was an emphasis on employee engagement and staff well-being. For example, Ernst & Young wants to treat employees in the same way as external customers – as an asset, not a cost. Its focus in employee engagement relates to this philosophy, as does its developing interest in the economics of happiness and well-being. One respondent at Ernst & Young described this as about getting the firm to 'fulfil its potential and that of its people'.

The former HR director of Hampshire County Council also talked of the importance of relating to employees. She hoped that this would be achieved in her organisation through the wellness programme it is developing. Other ideas to increase engagement at Hampshire County Council include developing clinics to inform employees of what HR does, but also so that they can see how business decisions are made and the rationale for them. This is part of an empowering agenda for staff. If they feel unable to control their own affairs, they will feel disengaged.

Alignment with business strategy

In light of the fact that the alignment between HR and business strategy has been part of the continuing debate on the purpose of HR (and was reflected in survey responses), it is not surprising that organisations focused on different strategic priorities. In line with Porter's typology (1985) of strategic alignment to reflect differentiation, focus or cost leadership, some align HR with business cost imperatives, whereas others are more concerned with quality or innovation.

The distinctive contribution of HR to business success can be seen in a number of different ways. Those organisations in which people are directly a source of competitive advantage are likely to focus on the quality or innovation end of the spectrum. So, for example, in a firm like Ernst & Young, with a high proportion of knowledge workers, there is special attention given to how innovation can be encouraged. This organisational positioning may be reflected in the employee brand or in the employment deal.

There can an alignment between CSR and branding. This is true in Capita's case. Their interest relates to the question of how to attract the right sort of recruits in a highly competitive labour market. This was consistent with other case-study views: CSR was regarded as an aspect of what the organisation stands for in a way that can be used to attract employees. It is therefore closely related to the employment brand. Moreover, reputation-building was the primary focus of CSR, either directly or indirectly, according to the CIPD research specifically on CSR (Reddington, 2005).

> '...our survey suggested that CSR is more of an issue for HR than branding. ...This poses the question of whether HR is only partly embracing the strategic role...'

Interestingly, our survey suggested that CSR is more of an issue for HR than branding. Only around a half of respondents had a role with respect to corporate branding compared with nearly three quarters who had some role in CSR. That may be because branding is still much more associated with corporate positioning than creating a distinctive recruitment proposition. This poses the question of whether HR is only partly embracing the strategic role if organisations do not see the importance of employer branding to recruitment and retention.

Cost efficiency

Lower on the list in the responses of survey respondents was the issue of costs. 'Cutting or controlling costs' was in last place on the list of main objectives, only identified by 16% of respondents as one of the top priorities. This is particularly interesting when compared with the results of the 2003 CIPD survey. Then 55% of the sample identified cutting costs as one of their priorities.

Cost management was given more prominence by some of our case-study interviewees. Ernst & Young expressed the view that HR should be delivering the people management strategy while simultaneously controlling costs. A Capita interviewee made a similar point about cost awareness, although more specifically within the HR remit and the impact on the business unit. The Hampshire County Council HR director emphasised that HR can demonstrate its value from a cost and risk perspective. Finally, Vodafone's strap-line for HR is 'high value, low cost'.

Administrative role

The feeling that emerged from the first stage of the research was that administrative activities were ones that HR had to get right if it were to add value at a more strategic level, but that many HR functions wished to reduce the administrative workload (through process improvement and automation) to free up time for these higher-level tasks. Indeed, some organisations were reported to be intent on 'getting rid' of administration as quickly as possible.

The survey suggests that there is progress in this regard. Three years ago the respondents reported that HR was spending half its time on HR activities, whereas now the figure was down to 38% and the expectation was that the proportion would fall to a quarter in three years' time. In support of the contention that administration is regarded to be of limited importance, only 5% of survey respondents thought that it was one of the three most important of HR tasks, yet half thought it was one of the three most time-consuming.

Of course, these objectives – to maintain administrative excellence but reduce time spent on such tasks – are not mutually contradictory. How this tension is resolved between the need to do administration, and do it well, and the desire to reduce its impact on the work of the function, varied between our case studies. At least at the level of rhetoric, some organisations wanted to reposition the function away from the administrative role. Irritation that some managers still pigeonholed HR as merely an administrative function, handling transactional matters, came through in some case studies. By contrast, other organisations reported that their goal was to deliver 'administrative excellence' and there was pride where the administrative infrastructure worked well, and was appreciated as such. A third response was to recognise that in many ways administrative tasks that had not been automated had become more complex and that the service standards were higher. This placed greater challenges on administrative staff than in the past.

Governance role

HR's governance role has a number of dimensions, covered below. It can be seen as ensuring that the organisation conforms to its legal obligations; is not at risk of infringing the law; is more broadly encouraging good people management practice; and is dealing with the outcome when such practice fails.

Securing compliance with employment regulations was important to 39% of survey respondents – somewhat higher than the 31% in 2003. This might reflect further employment legislation in the last four years. In some of the case-study discussions, this simple need for compliance became a richer imperative of risk management – ensuring that the organisation retains its reputation and lives its values. HR as the 'conscience' of the organisation (Ernst & Young) is perhaps a different – and maybe more acceptable – way of articulating the employee champion role. It perhaps emphasises the need for HR to protect employees from poor people management practice. It also moves HR away from being solely a 'support' or 'advisory' function, as was articulated by many survey participants.

The debate about this aspect of HR's role is illustrated by the use of the 'policeman' term. At Capita, HR did not want to be seen as adopting this role, nor did its line customers (as the earlier quote indicates). The role HR performs in this sort of organisation is to explain the implications (legal or otherwise) of a particular course of action that is being considered. It is then up to the management to decide how they manage the risk.

> '...that HR has a "policeman" role...is a more cautious approach – less one of risk management and more one aimed at risk avoidance.'

By contrast, interviewees at Hampshire County Council accepted that HR has a policeman role because management 'looks to us to make sure [the line] meets legislation'. This is a more cautious approach – less one of risk management and more one aimed at risk avoidance. Indeed, on this subject there appears to be a difference between the private sector and the public. According to the survey, a higher proportion of public sector respondents than private sector described compliance with employment regulations as a key objective.

IMPLICATIONS

One should not expect to obtain a neat answer to the question of the role and purpose of HR from research such as this. It is, as we have said, a long-standing debate and is likely to continue. Nevertheless, several emerging themes can be highlighted.

Firstly, Ulrich's employee champion role really does not seem to have been embraced, and the administrative expert role seems to produce a mixed reaction. The emphasis in most organisations seems to be on the top half of his quadrant (Figure 1 on page 3) – strategic partner and change agent. HR still has to ensure that administration is done well, but it does not want the volume of this activity to inhibit its strategic role. Equally, the fact that HR is not keen on the employee champion concept does not mean that HR has lost interest in employees, but that in large organisations, at least, it does not interact with them as individuals but in a collective form only. HR is increasingly interested in employee engagement, commitment and motivation, and how these link to organisational performance. Moreover, there seems to be growing interest in CSR and employee 'wellness'.

The second theme is that HR's contribution not only divides along the familiar operational/strategic axis but also along a delivery/facilitating axis. Thus, in the bottom left part of Figure 3, HR is providing systems, procedures and policies as the people management infrastructure within which HR operates. The service delivery work may often be operational, but – as we saw with companies like Capita and Fujitsu – these activities can become very strategic and commercial in nature.

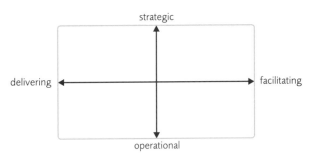

Figure 3 ❖ The elements of HR's contribution

Source: CIPD (2007)

On the right-hand side of the model, HR may be facilitating change and helping managers discharge their people management responsibilities. This may move from generic coaching of the line to more active encouragement. HR's facilitation of employee engagement is at organisations like Vodafone truly strategic because of the business impact that can result from managers energising the workforce.

There is a still in the HR community an emphasis placed on the strategic and business-aligned contribution of the function. This came through in the survey. Participants were asked where they sit in the operational-to-strategic continuum. In general, they saw the function as more operational than strategic. The majority felt that the function was business-driven (even more than in 2003) and able to offer tailored solutions to business problems. The key point, however, is that the respondents wanted to shift the function towards being more strategic and proactive, and a good proportion thought they were 'getting there'.

Yet there are still many organisations that seem, from the written survey responses, to wish to limit themselves to a support role only. The box below offers a selection of responses to the question on the primary role of HR.

❖ To provide managers with employment law/policy guidance and advice. To support organisational change.

❖ To support the business in achieving its objectives.

❖ To support and sustain the business in every respect.

❖ To ensure compliance with legislation, support of managers, support of the business.

❖ To provide a day-to-day operational HR function for the organisation and support the core business objectives.

❖ To generate and support the right people in the right roles to benefit the company.

❖ To support managers in the discharge of their operational and managerial responsibility.

❖ To provide managers with operational support. To provide policy development and support.

❖ To see to the administration of the HR function. To provide legal advice and support and guidance.

There is nothing wrong with HR playing a support role, as our earlier discussion indicated. If this is all that HR feels it can do, there is the possibility that the relationship with management becomes akin to that between a master and servant, or, at least, a customer and a service supplier. The difficulty with this positioning is that it suggests that HR is there to do management's bidding in a situation where the customer is always right.

Some organisations have tried to avoid this situation. Cable and Wireless, for example, explicitly moved from a support role to one in which challenge was seen as legitimate. This was a key way in which the function was able to add business value. The description, at Ernst & Young, of HR as the 'conscience' of the organisation gives it more of a guardian's role, similar to the 'regulator' description used by Storey (1992) that implies it has a governance function. The function is to uphold organisational values by acting to stop those that fail to operate by them. This gives HR a right to intervene if there is discrimination, harassment, sexual impropriety, corruption, etc. In some organisations, this responsibility is formally invested in HR. In others, it is assumed and accepted. The critical point is that HR has a role independent of line management. It may provide services and be customer-centric in so doing. It may respond to business needs as described by line colleagues. However, it also acts independently to protect people who are a vital asset of the organisation. As Neil Roden, HR director at RBS (quoted in Reilly and Williams, 2006), puts it:

HR is right at times to interfere in the employment relationship. It can't afford line managers screwing up on precious talent.

If you take this line, then HR is not the servant to the management's master but an equal business partner, or as Wendy Hirsh puts it, a 'business champion' (Hirsh *et al*, forthcoming), questioning the line's view of employees for the benefit of the organisation as a whole.

Further, there is a link to risk management – protecting the organisation from mistakes in relation to employees who might damage it, but also judging when the business imperative has to be followed. The CIPD report on risk management (CIPD, 2006d) rightly distinguishes between risk management and risk avoidance. It seems from the evidence presented by this earlier research that HR is better at identifying people management risks (including that of management behaviour, as well as, among other things, reputation, legal compliance, skills shortages) than at contributing to the wider, organisational risk agenda. Perhaps the people management orientation is understandable, but we would argue that HR should be aiming to become more of a risk manager. In so doing, HR should be solution-focused, not a problem-identifier. It should be finding acceptable and appropriate ways for managers to meet business goals without compromising on organisational values or vital assets.

> '...we would argue that HR should be aiming to become more of a risk manager. In so doing, HR should be...finding acceptable and appropriate ways for managers to meet business goals...'

The role of HR as risk manager and the nature of the value it delivers are affected by the way it interacts with line management and where it sits on the two axes we presented in Figure 3. HR must beware lest, by adopting a support role and eschewing direct contact with employees, it becomes both passive and distant from the organisation, limiting its 'doing' to offering a policy infrastructure and letting the line get on with the people management activity. The management of risk then transfers almost entirely to the line.

A more active, interventionist approach by HR may be characterised as acting like a policeman by managers, but it might be a better means by which risk is identified and dealt with, especially if it is put in the framework of employee engagement. Overly focusing on strategy may also mean that HR is not sufficiently cognisant of the day-to-day execution of people management – but equally, operational work without a strategic focus has the danger of being too short-term and reactive.

Finally, the different emphasis given by research participants in the types of value HR offers varies in part with the area of HR activity that is being considered. For example, the value basis of OD is different from that of payroll. It varies with the nature of the organisation and its value proposition to the market. What is valued will also be affected by those that interact with the function. As Ulrich and colleagues state in a forthcoming article, 'The vision of value is revealed through the perception of each stakeholder' (Ulrich *et al*, forthcoming).

The different ways in which value presents itself was emphasised to us by Mike Watts, then Director HR

Transformation, Cabinet Office. He offers a value typology (shown in Figure 4) that illustrates that HR's value-adding can be achieved through efficient administration and operational excellence; through enabling business change; by facilitating strategic choice; and by building organisational capability.

These distinctions are consistent with the operational/strategic, service delivery/facilitating axes we noted from the research responses. They also fit the argument advanced by the CIPD report on change management: 'Strategic HR does not operate in a different sphere from the technical: they are mutually complementary' (Whittington and Molloy, 2005). Finally, which of these value elements predominates will be affected by the business model, as described earlier. In a simple public sector/private sector split, it is interesting to note that the public sector gives more attention to compliance and diversity; the private sector emphasises employee engagement and employee alignment with business goals.

Figure 4 ❖ HR's value contribution

HR provides value for money	HR adds value for money
HR creates value	HR delivers value

Source: CIPD (2007)

LEARNING POINTS

❖ HR should be clear about the multiple roles it plays. It should work out how it adds value in different ways and not confuse the different types of proposition and how it measures them:

   ❖ As a deliverer of services (administrative and operational) it needs to be efficient and effective in terms of business requirements.

   ❖ As a facilitator of the line people management role, it should coach and support consistent with personal requirements and the business context.

   ❖ As the conscience of the organisation, HR should play a governance role to uphold corporate values, even if it does not (generally) get involved in the day-to-day people management.

   ❖ As a risk manager, HR should be judging when to intervene to prevent reputational or financial damage to the organisation. It should go beyond problem identification to offering problem solutions.

   ❖ As leader of people management, HR should exercise a corporate duty to nurture the whole employee resource. This means having an independent view from the line of what engages (and disengages) employees and being able to develop and apply appropriate methods of engaging them.

❖ Combining these contributions, HR can be both the strategic player it seeks to be, and also the supporter of managers and employees that its customers want it to be.

STRUCTURE

❖ **There are a variety of HR organisational forms but the three-legged stool model is the most common, although there are many variations to it.**

❖ **Enabling the HR function to be a more strategic contributor emerged as the top reason for structural change in our survey.**

❖ **Business partners are the most commonly-found group. An equal number of organisations have centres of expertise and shared services.**

❖ **Although benefits in service quality, in customer responsiveness, and in the credibility of HR have been particularly reported after introducing the three-legged stool, problems stem from a segmented service delivery model.**

INTRODUCTION

Much of the debate about HR transformation has centred on restructuring the function, introducing some form of the so-called Ulrich or three-legged stool model. Figure 5 describes the standard format – the centres of expertise, shared service centres and business partners being the three 'legs', and, rather confusingly, the corporate centre a fourth element.

The three-legged stool approach is deemed to be most attractive for larger organisations, which are more complex and have greater degrees of specialisation. However, this has taken on the form of a 'best practice' design, which can be applied irrespective of circumstances. The experts interviewed for our earlier report expressed frustration with what they saw as a fixation with one particular model, arguing that HR's structure should reflect the business it is in and what business customers want – a 'best fit' approach. Michael Porter has long since argued that structure should follow strategy, an approach that is supported by Ulrich, who believes that HR will take one of three general forms (Ulrich and Brockbank, 2005):

Figure 5 ❖ **The 'three-legged stool' HR structure**

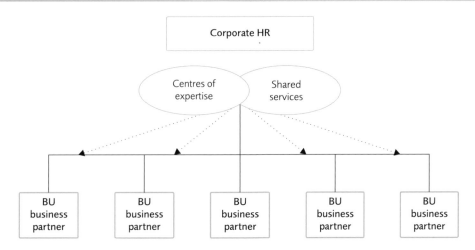

Source: CIPD survey (2007)

Note: This is the so-called Ulrich model because although his name is associated with it, he did not describe this structure. Indeed, he has also commented that the three-legged stool description is a misnomer: it should be four-legged to include the corporate centre. In a forthcoming article he reviews this issue, proposing the addition of an operational execution leg.

- ❖ HR functional organisation, with specialists providing both theory and practice, aligned to a single business

- ❖ HR shared services organisation, aligned to a diversified business

- ❖ embedded HR, aligned to a business unit of a holding company as dedicated HR.

This more sophisticated model suggests a more differentiated approach. It takes account not just of business strategy in shaping the HR structure but also the configuration of the organisation's business structure (centralised or decentralised). The size, sector and maturity of organisations might also play a part in shaping the form of the HR structure.

The seeming rush to adopt 'Ulrich' is despite some evidence that *sustained* cost reductions may not be achieved by the move to shared service operations (PriceWaterhouseCoopers, 2006). Further, there have been criticisms of remote experts delivering gold-plated but business-illiterate policies, and of business partners becoming the opposite – too embedded within their business unit to see the importance of the organisation overall. There have also been criticisms of the segmentation of the whole service delivery model, on the basis that it can result in issues falling between the cracks and can lead to a more complex system of customer service. (See Reilly and Williams, 2006, for further details of these criticisms.)

RESEARCH RESULTS

Figure 6 and Figure 7 guide readers through the responses to questions on structural change.

As can be seen, the vast majority (81%) of survey respondents had changed their HR model, and an even higher proportion of these had done so within the past three years. Of those that had reorganised, only 57% had opted for the so called Ulrich model in some shape or form, an equal number adopting it partly and in full. Of the 42% that had not chosen the three-legged stool model or a variant of it, as Figure 7, opposite, shows, two thirds used the traditional single HR team combining HR administrators, specialists and generalists in one team. Almost all the rest had a corporate HR team with decentralised operational teams, organised by business unit or location.

The survey questionnaire concentrated thereafter on the three legs of the model, so we have no more detail on these other organisational forms, except to observe that they were more likely to be found, as expected, in smaller organisations.

As to what constitutes the three legs of the model, the theory is plain: there should be centres of expertise, business partners and shared services. In fact, although 29% claimed that their HR function had been restructured to reflect the full model, cross-tabulating the results to the individual questions on the 'three legs' shows that in fact only 18% of respondents' organisations had shared services, business partners and centres of expertise. One can speculate as to why some organisations reported that they had the full model but not all three components of it, but it certainly reinforces the impression that the pure model is not as common as the publicity that surrounds it, nor as well understood.

Our case study research was with large organisations – with the exception of one, the organisational form of which is described in the box opposite.

Figure 6 ❖ The range of structural change

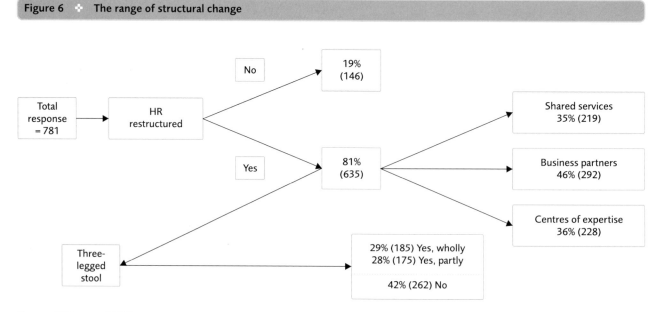

Source: CIPD survey (2007)

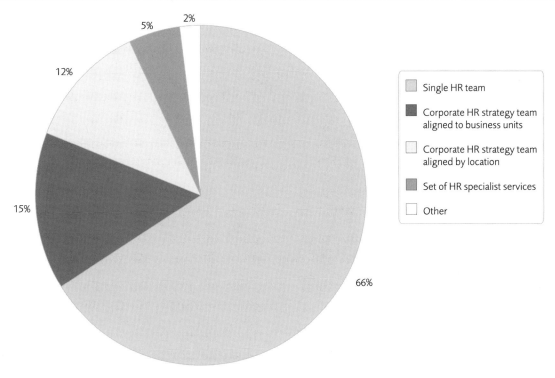

Figure 7 ❖ **Structures of the HR function other than the 'Ulrich model'**

Legend:
- Single HR team
- Corporate HR strategy team aligned to business units
- Corporate HR strategy team aligned by location
- Set of HR specialist services
- Other

2%, 5%, 12%, 15%, 66%

Source: CIPD survey (2007)

Firefly, a PR company with around 50 employees, largely in London but with offices in other European capitals, has a simple HR function. The CEO acts as head of the function, but there is an HR manager who is a real generalist. She helps define the HR strategy so that it is aligned with the business plan and looks after recruitment and retention, compensation and benefits, training and development, employment law, policy and procedures, internal communication and counselling. She gets some support from the directors' PA on administrative work.

The other case studies operated some form of three-legged stool model, but as with the survey results, we discovered a number where there had been partial implementation.

Indeed, we found many variations on the textbook model. For example:

❖ a large number of business partners and a shared service centre, but no centres of expertise because business partners are expected to be conversant with most HR issues

❖ a small number of business partners – one for each department – a policy unit, a separate learning and development design unit, a call centre, a 'duty desk' casework section and a project team; administration is carried out by shared service centres located outside HR

❖ a corporate HR function, an insourced shared services operation and a well-staffed business unit HR

❖ business partners for each of the main departments and centres of excellence, including an employment support line, which pick up the administrative work; there is a shared payroll operation but no shared service centre as such

❖ shared services (where appropriate, globally), business partners (aligned to global business units, regions or individual locations) and centres of excellence

❖ business partners, an advisory call centre, a global shared service centre, and different levels of centres of expertise at global (principles and strategy), regional (guidance on implementation) and local level (actual delivery)

❖ business partners, together with learning and development advisers embedded in business units, with a corporate 'service delivery' unit and a strategy and consultancy group

❖ a small number of HR teams, led by a business partner, a support unit/shared service centre and a policy and strategy unit

- business partners, regional administrative service centres, together with call centres, but with payroll executed locally; no centres of expertise, but 'core HR strategy' units and 'delivery teams'.

(More detail on these structures in the main case-study organisations can be found in Appendix 2.)

What is evident from the above is that shared service centres in some form or another (but usually including a call centre and transaction processing) are to be found in most of our main case studies; centres of expertise are present in many organisations but in various formats; and business partners feature in all our case studies (except Firefly). There are also additional elements (eg delivery teams or case management units) involved in operational HR. Our case studies tended to be large and complex organisations, which would explain the prevalence of shared services. Some parts of the shared service activity might be outsourced or insourced (by being carried out by another part of the organisation), but it is the pulling together of administrative activities that is most common.

HR shared services

Of the survey organisations that had in some way introduced the 'Ulrich' model, two thirds had HR shared services. As previously mentioned, shared services is a large organisation phenomenon rather than small: two thirds of organisations that employ 5,000 or more employees have a service centre, compared with only 17% of the 250 to 1,000 category.

> '...two thirds of organisations that employ 5,000 or more employees have a service centre...'

Among our case studies, some had gone straight to shared services; others had taken longer, seeking to sort out their processes first. The decision to introduce shared services seemed in most organisations to be driven primarily by cost, efficiency and headcount considerations. The change programme and process re-engineering required to extract transactional activities from departments/locations was reported to be complex and a 'huge' effort by some organisations.

The question of whether shared services should be outsourced or done in house is dealt with in Chapter 5.

Business partners

The survey results partly bear out the prevalence of business partners as reported in other research: 83% of the survey organisations that had in some way introduced the 'Ulrich' model have business partners.

Among our case studies it was possible to see that the business partner structure varies in form. In particular, there is difference in terms of whether business partners operate as solo operators or as part of a business partnering team, their number (relative to the rest of HR), and whether they report to the business unit or to HR. The following examples are taken from our case study organisations.

- Ernst & Young, for example, has HR business partners based in the business, but it also has learning and development/talent management advisers for each of its business groups.

- The six business partners at Hampshire County Council have some additional resource to help them with operational delivery. They also report to the business head.

- At HMRC, the business partners report to their business unit heads but with a dotted line to the head of business partnering, who in turn reports to the Head of Strategy and Consultancy. This is because the organisation wants business partners to be involved in strategy formulation to ensure that the business voice is heard and so that the business partners adhere to corporate policy.

- In the initial phase of MOD's HR transformation, 490 posts were identified to support HR at business level. This reflected the MOD's geographical dispersion, its devolved organisational model and its diverse client base. Subsequent review has refined the numbers and original roles – in particular in the light of the full introduction of shared service operation and the experience of meeting the real needs of the business.

- Capita has 44 business partners, structured to support each division for Sales, Integration and Operational activities. The HR team ultimately reports to the Group HR director.

> 'The better the case management system (and...people management) support, the more likely that business partners will be able to focus on strategic change.'

Thus we can contrast those organisations (like Ernst & Young and Hampshire County Council) that have small numbers of business partners with those that have larger numbers (eg MOD or Capita). Where organisations have a relatively large number of business partners, one issue that could make a difference is if their role is not a purely strategic one, but heavily involved in operational support. Relevant here is how the level of central case management support bears on the business partner role. The better the case management system (and, indeed, the operational people management) support, the more likely that business partners will be able to focus on strategic change. If case management (and operational support) is weak, then business partners 'get dragged in' to individual employee or line manager issues. As one embedded HR team member explained, there was 'often not the time to go to a board meeting' because of the pressure of other work. One response to this challenge has been to add assistant business partners or embedded HR advisers to deal with case or operational work.

How much operational work is carried out by business partners is also affected by the stage of development of the HR model and how HR conceives the business partner role, and also the relationship to the line. At Capita, HR managers do not get into the detail, because the line is relatively self-sufficient, but they are responsive to what the business wants without being concerned about whether it is strategic or operational. Companies that operate internationally report that they are adjusting their UK model to suit local circumstances. Reuters is one organisation that makes the point that business needs, not the purity of the structure, is what drives how HR is organised. Business partners may get involved in operational work if the business needs require it. This is not the prime function of the role, but business partners are not expected to be precious about what they do. The term 'business partnering' as a philosophy is in this situation more appropriate than 'business partner' as a role.

The opposite alternative is to have a small number of business partners who are instructed to take a tough line with managers and route queries or requests for help to the shared service centre, so that they are not distracted from their primary role of strategic contribution to organisational success.

As for reporting lines: as we have seen, some organisations operate like E.ON where the HR managers report to HR with a dotted line to the business unit head. Others again, like Ernst & Young and Hampshire County Council, report to business unit heads. The choice of approach may reflect either the desire for the business partners to be engaged with their business colleagues as full members of the business unit management team or the wish for HR to retain a strong influence over their work. It is not clear whether those that conceive the business partner role more narrowly are also more likely to report to the business unit head than to HR.

Centres of expertise

As in the case of shared services, two thirds of organisations with a three-legged structure have centres of expertise, more often in the private than public sector. However, the case studies revealed that in practice there was real divergence over whether or not organisations have centres of expertise at all, and then some variation in form where they do.

'...there was real divergence over whether or not organisations have centres of expertise at all, and then some variation in form where they do.'

There are different structural responses where there are no centres of expertise. The first option is to locate HR expertise in the business unit. The reasoning is that corporate centres of expertise are too remote and specific business unit knowledge is needed to be effective. Thus, in financial services the reward strategy for the retail business could be different from that for investment banking. A second option locates expertise in the corporate centre. Here, subject matter policy development is undertaken. This is exemplified by Capita. Capita's business partners are expected to be more self-reliant in terms of expertise, but in a role that puts a lot of emphasis on consultancy or delivery – more on policy implementation or adaptation than development. Similarly, in Fujitsu Services there is no need for separate expertise units in many locations because the HR managers are all-rounders and the cost would probably not seem to be justified.

The conventional centres of expertise were to be seen at Ernst & Young, with both a policy role and a reference point for queries, whereas Vodafone, HMRC, Hampshire County Council, Nortel and Surrey County Council all have some form of expertise unit, but the reference point for queries was located elsewhere. In Surrey County Council, Nortel and HMRC, centres of expertise are explicitly policy units. Vodafone has different types of centres of expertise by geography, and Hampshire County Council, unusually, combines policy with administration. (More detail on these examples is to be found in Appendix 2.)

The size of organisations has an effect on whether separate centres of expertise make sense. In smaller organisations (including multinational subsidiaries) there is much more multi-tasking. For example, Nortel has more 'double-hatting' in some of its smaller countries, where HR performs the tasks of business partner and operational delivery. Similarly, local HR managers in Fujitsu Services also cover a wide range of activities – transactional, operational support, consultancy, etc. They are supported by HR specialists who may look after a business unit or geographical area, together with an area of subject matter expertise. For example, the reward specialist at Fujitsu also covers continental Europe as a geographic area.

Case management and operational HR

As we have seen, a key debate around the role of HR is whether or not HR becomes involved in the day-to-day management of people. In many cases HR's role is the indirect one of setting people management policies and the provision of training for managers in their practice. The difficulty then is to decide how HR should respond where the line cannot cope. Response to this situation varied. As with some other organisations, HMRC has casework as part of its shared services operation. Interestingly, HMRC has added two extra strands. It has 'mobile advisers' to support managers face to face where the case is particularly complex or serious and where help over the phone is insufficient. It also has a 'taskforce', the role of which is to bring managers up to speed with the development of HR policy and practice. The MOD also has deployable case support officers as part of its comprehensive service model.

Surrey County Council has a specific case work unit to deal with problems referred to it by the duty desk and by business partners. It has cut back on the number of business partners such that they have to be selective in what they do and rely upon these centrally provided services.

In organisations like Capita there is less operational work for HR to do because there is a high expectation of what line management will cover in terms of dealing with their people problems. Their self-reliance affects the business partner role.

Much of the casework seems to be supporting line managers in dealing with difficult disciplinary or absence cases, although Vodafone highlighted how its call centre picks up and deals with a lot of individual, employee enquiries.

Delivery units can also be used by organisations as one way of ensuring that HR policy turns into practice. In other words, another leg is added to the stool. For example, at Vodafone

line managers can directly contact the recruitment centre of expertise and technical training is separately organised for each business unit. Nortel also ensures that implementation of policy is effected through delivery units.

Drivers of change

When asked what drove the change in HR structure, the desire to enable the HR function to be a more strategic contributor came out top in our survey, as shown in Table 1 below. The need to improve service standards and increase business focus came next, while cost reduction came fourth, identified by only 29% of respondents. The other answers reinforce a picture of HR in charge of its restructuring. Only 10% said they were responding to line demands, and a quarter of respondents agreed there was a need to fit wider organisational change.

> '...the desire to enable the HR function to be a more strategic contributor came out top in our survey...'

These results suggest that HR wants to put its house in order and move more towards a situation where it is adding value in the way it wants, rather than being driven by either customers or wider organisational change. At the Dublin discussion group, the less charitable explanation was given that HR was merely following fashion in adopting the 'Ulrich' structure and that it was an 'HR solution for HR'.

Table 1 ✥ Change drivers in restructuring	
	%
Change due to cost reduction	29
Change due to a need to improve services	34
Change due to a need for more responsive services	23
Change due to repositioning the HR function	24
Change due to HR becoming a more strategic contributor	52
Change due to improving credibility of function	19
Change due to line demands for changed service	10
Change due to increased business focus	30
Change due to a need to fit wider organisational model	24
Change due to another reason	6

Source: CIPD survey (2007)
Note: Multiple answers were possible to the series of questions that evoked these responses.

THE CHANGING HR FUNCTION

The survey feedback also contrasts with a Deloitte report (2005) that 70% of early adopters of the 'Ulrich' model did so primarily to save money. Certainly, this was a very strong motivation in both our private sector and public sector case-study organisations. In the latter, external pressures like the Gershon review, best value reviews or internal drivers of organisational cost reduction had a major impact. In the private sector examples there is a sense of a relentless drive for improved efficiency. Vodafone UK, for example, had reduced costs and HR headcount by a third to make for a leaner and more effective function. Nortel cut about 18% of the jobs in global HR in the two years between January 2005 and January 2007, and half-way through this journey two thirds of the function changed jobs. These developments have been significantly affected by extending the reach of shared services and cutting out the role of HR advisers that carried out a lot of operational HR tasks.

This is not to say that there were not other considerations – as the Nortel box, below, implies. Both the local government case studies wanted greater adherence to corporate policy and more consistency in service delivery that would be an improvement on the variety in service quality and content that was experienced in the previous decentralised structure which gave departments much more freedom in HR policy and practice. Hampshire County Council, for example, found itself with 174 grades that it has now been able to reduce to 11. Vodafone is also keen to obtain greater consistency, but this is in a global context. The expectation is that if all the operating companies work to a common approach to HR, it makes it much easier to compare performance between companies. At Fujitsu Services the pressure to progress from the previous Ulrich-style model is driven by the HR director, but with the focus on how HR can efficiently and effectively support the evolving business. Since the company's activities grow rapidly through the outsourcing deals it wins, the organisational shape is in constant flux and HR has to find a flexible approach to match.

The HR 'evolution' objectives at Nortel were defined as:

❖ simplify and standardise global processes

❖ simplify employee data capture

❖ reduce HR operating costs

❖ improve the quality of HR services

❖ further automate/centralise HR shared services

❖ improve employee efficiency through self-service

❖ improve manager efficiency and increase accountability through self-service

---

❖ enable HR to be more strategic

❖ leverage existing IT investment

❖ create a more integrated technology platform.

Structural problems

Inevitably, new structures bring new problems. Phase 1 of the project highlighted a number of issues that the survey was able to explore in more depth.

We asked about the challenges of operating the three-legged stool model. The results bear out the evidence from Phase 1 of this project – in particular that organisational segmentation is a significant problem that needs to be addressed if HR structural transformation is to be successful:

❖ Introducing shared services has produced boundary problems (identified by 56% of respondents), gaps in service provision (41%) and communication difficulties (36%).

❖ The difficulty of separating out transactional work from the activities of specialists (46%) was the principal problem with centres of expertise, followed by communication with the rest of the function (34%).

❖ 'Getting drawn into the "wrong" activities' was the number one challenge with business partners (49%), with the tension between corporate and business unit needs a close second (46%).

These responses were illustrated by interviewees. One HR team member said of his new HR model, 'We have replaced one set of silos [based on business units] with another [based on HR functions].' Another organisation reported that the shared service centre was not engaging well with the business customer, in a situation where the business partners were of variable quality.

Structural solutions

The challenge is to overcome these problems of difficult communication, unclear interfaces or role definitions that lead to gaps or overlaps.

> '...organisations need someone who can pull ...a disparate team together and prevent cracks in the structure from becoming gaping holes.'

STRUCTURE

We discussed with our case studies some potential solutions. The importance of leadership was identified as central to success by an HR manager at Ernst & Young. He suggested that 'the Ulrich model holds together better where there is power at the centre'. In other words, organisations need someone who can pull what can be a disparate team together and prevent cracks in the structure from becoming gaping holes.

Other case-study participants pointed to the quality of interaction as a key element in developing an effective model. Vodafone reported that the trust between business partners and the centres of expertise allowed the model to work. There was mutual respect and the fact that the staff are both at the same grade avoided the problem reported elsewhere that business partners are perceived to look down on their HR colleagues. At Ernst & Young there was a good debate now between business partners and centres of expertise on policy development, rather than siloed thinking. Moreover, business partners were no longer required to know everything about HR. It has become acceptable to refer managers to the centres of expertise.

The benefits of structural change

As for the benefits identified, the survey asked for views on each leg of the structure. Most of the benefits related to the drivers for change. Thus, to around a third of organisations (for whom multiple answers were possible to the questions posed), shared services offered 'major' improvements in service quality, customer responsiveness, and the credibility of HR, and success in the repositioning of the function and making it more strategic. Cost reduction only provided 'some' change for 60% of respondents. The benefits of the business partner role centred again on HR becoming more of a strategic contributor (76%), with increased business focus (69%) and greater line engagement and people management issues higher on the agenda (both 60%). Centres of expertise have delivered benefits in terms of deeper professional expertise (69%), and again in terms of HR becoming more of a strategic contributor (56%). Higher-quality advice to business partners and greater consistency of advice were chosen by over half the respondents.

Evidence of change

An interesting question is whether these perceptions are shared by customers and can be demonstrated through more detailed evaluation. If this sounds a touch sceptical, it is because of the Lawler *et al* research (2003) reported in the earlier project report (CIPD, 2006a), which suggested that structural change did not necessarily bring the expected benefits in strategic repositioning. This study can throw some light on this subject by looking at respondents' perceptions of the proportion of time the HR function is spending on strategic input compared with operational and administrative activities.

The survey suggests that HR staff have cut by a quarter the amount of time they spend on administration compared with

three years ago, and more or less doubled the amount of time devoted to strategic matters. The proportion of time spent on operational work has remained constant during this period, amounting to around 40% of their time.

It is interesting that the type of restructure has had no effect on these results – ie whether a three-legged stool has been introduced (partly or in full) or not makes little difference to these figures.

> Nortel undertook activity analysis before the company embarked on its HR evolution. It divided its work into four categories – strategy, performance enhancement, transactions, and administration. It then looked at these dimensions from the perspectives of 'field/line' HR, corporate HR and the HR shared service centre. The field HR team were at that point spending over a third of their time on transactions and administration, and corporate HR was devoting a similar proportion of its time to performance enhancement. The aim of its evolution is for corporate HR to spend the bulk of its time on strategic issues; for the shared service centre to utilise the same proportion of time on transactions and administration; and for the field HR to focus on performance enhancement.

Another clue comes from the activities on which these senior HR survey respondents are spending their time, as shown in Figure 8, opposite, which shows the percentage of respondents who listed activity areas as among the three most important/most time-consuming. Half the survey respondents identified HR administration as one of three most time-consuming activities, and nearly three quarters identified supporting line managers. By comparison, change management was chosen by a third, developing HR strategy and policy by 28% and working on business strategy by only 14%.

This contrasts with views on what are the three most important activities, where developing HR strategy and policy is seen the top item (64%), followed by contributing to business strategy (58%). Providing specialist HR input and change management was identified as most important by half of the survey's respondents. HR administration, as we have reported, only received votes from 5% of respondents.

Looking back to 2003, these survey results are comparable. Given the somewhat different composition of the respondents, the similarity on the key dimensions of time spent versus importance for business strategy and HR administration is striking.

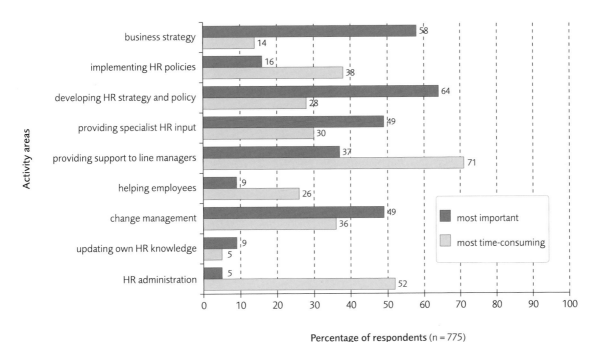

Figure 8 ❖ The three most important/most time-consuming activities

Activity areas:
- business strategy: most important 58, most time-consuming 14
- implementing HR policies: most important 16, most time-consuming 38
- developing HR strategy and policy: most important 64, most time-consuming 28
- providing specialist HR input: most important 49, most time-consuming 30
- providing support to line managers: most important 37, most time-consuming 71
- helping employees: most important 9, most time-consuming 26
- change management: most important 49, most time-consuming 36
- updating own HR knowledge: most important 9, most time-consuming 5
- HR administration: most important 5, most time-consuming 52

Legend: ■ most important ▪ most time-consuming

Percentage of respondents (n = 775)

Source: CIPD survey (2007)

IMPLICATIONS

In considering the implications of these findings there are several areas to examine: the sort of HR structures that have been implemented and why; the process of change; problems encountered and benefits realised; the relative importance of structural change; and what might be the new ideas in structural change. We cover these points in the sections below.

Choice of structure

The picture that emerges from this research is that structural change has been widely chosen to reposition the function, but by no means has this all focused on the three-legged stool model of HR. There has been a real concern expressed by practitioners that too many organisations have rushed headlong into an 'Ulrich' model without seeing whether it addressed the organisational needs. The risk with this approach is that the model is not owned, or indeed understood, by the top team (an issue we will return to in Chapter 10). As one contributor at the Dublin discussion group put it: it has become 'a badge of honour' to introduce this structure.

There may be some truth in this statement, although the survey and case studies produce a more nuanced picture. Where the so-called Ulrich structure has been introduced, there have been many variations in its form. Business partners are the most common feature; centres of expertise and shared service centres less so. There are also delivery or casework

units, strategy and policy groups. The positive aspect of this response is that many organisations seem to have heeded the suggestions of our survey contributors who expressed variations on the following recommendation: 'The Ulrich model is useful – but adapt it to your circumstances.'

> '...many organisations seem to have heeded...our survey contributors who expressed variations on the following recommendation: "The Ulrich model is useful – but adapt it to your circumstances."'

Structure follows strategy ...

The other perhaps more important message that emerges from this research is that there is no one model that neatly fits all circumstances. As one HR manager argues: 'Structure is only a tool like any other tool.' Ulrich himself did not design the structure attributed to him, and his advice is that structure should follow strategy. If one conceives of strategy in a broad sense (including the size and maturity of the organisation and how its business model operates), then this must be right. But it is also true that separating out generalist business-aligned HR from deep expertise makes a lot of sense, not least in skill terms. Similarly, segmenting transactional work from transformational has merit, particularly through protecting time to be devoted to the latter. Combining activities that can reasonably be shared has enormous economies of scale benefits if the size and dispersed nature of operations justifies it and getting staff to concentrate on what they are good at helps improve service quality.

Dealing with structural problems

There are therefore genuine reasons for adopting a three-legged stool approach to HR structure. What we have also seen is that there are potential pitfalls that have to be addressed. Firstly, the model has its faults in segmentation of service delivery, awkward communication across structural boundaries and complex customer interfaces. One of the other perceived problems of the three-legged stool model that derives from its segmentation is the so called 'polo' problem (Reilly and Williams, 2006). This refers to the gap in service provision between the three legs of the structure. Managers may find themselves unable to successfully execute people management tasks (eg in hiring or development) and cannot call upon business partners (who see their role as strategic), centres of expertise (who see their role in terms of policy formulation or advice) or shared service centres (that are concerned with administrative tasks).

What organisations have to do (and in many cases are doing) is to blur the edges of the model so that communication is enhanced and cracks are covered over, rather than assume that managers are more self-sufficient than they really are. Those organisations that give operational support to managers are dealing head-on with this issue, whether through delivery or casework units or through business partnering teams.

Flexibility in service delivery

Another way to modify the service delivery model is to move away from a single method that applies to all business units. We did not get many comments about how the twin objectives of efficiency and effectiveness that should drive service delivery can be met. Previous research (eg Reilly and Williams, 2006) has highlighted the fact that organisations that have offered a vanilla service delivery model, introduced primarily to save costs and not to respond to customer needs, have faced complaints about the 'one-size-fits-all' approach. Some organisations have responded by being more flexible on some aspects of the service (eg business units can choose to use the central recruitment service or not, but they cannot develop their own payroll system). Hampshire County Council reported, for example, having more discussions with customers about what they want. But there are limits to how far HR can go. As an HR manager from Capita said: 'It is impossible to have a tailored service delivered efficiently.'

The push towards being customer-responsive and adaptable comes at a price. Is the organisation willing to pay, or do managers find it easier to moan about the downsides of standardisation without acknowledging the benefits?

> 'The push towards being customer-responsive and adaptable comes at a price'

The argument we make on the basis of the research is that this decision should be self-conscious and in line with business imperatives, not with HR fashions. It should relate to the business model – from where does competitive advantage come? There are options at both ends of the flexibility/efficiency spectrum so that organisations can choose less standardisation and more business unit freedom to operate in their own way or the opposite. The choice will affect the size and cost of the HR function, but also the nature of its impact on the strategic/operational and on the service delivery/facilitation axes.

Deciding where the organisation should be on this continuum should be the outcome of a more open-ended debate with customers than seems often to be the case.

Structure in international context

There is a similar discussion for those case studies operating on a global basis on the degree of consolidation that is desirable or possible: how much variation to a common, global model should there be, and how much local difference should be accepted? There is a balance to be struck between the benefits of economies of scale and the need to be sensitive to local differences and practicalities (eg employment regulation or compensation and benefits systems). How to strike this balance partly depends on organisational preferences – history and the business model might point towards or against centralisation – but it is also a matter of scale. As the RBS example box below shows, smaller organisations (and the definition of 'smaller' will vary) are much harder to corral into a common model. Getting an HR unit to fit into the standard format might not be worth the effort, especially if there are language differences (affecting the call centre) or terms and conditions are unusual (affecting payroll). As some of our interviewees reported, corporate change programmes can encounter 'push back' from local operating companies that believe their cultural and legal circumstances are unique and that remote service centres will not provide an adequate service.

> RBS does not operate a single global template that must be adhered to anywhere in the world. European and Asian businesses, below approximately 5,000 employees, do not form part of the shared services operation because there is currently insufficient scale. The business case to move to shared services is not

strong enough compared to other investments available to the Bank. This approach differs from other large organisations such as Unilever and Citigroup, where there is one model without exception. The business case for a single model is that the overall savings made from commonality outweigh the absence of savings, or indeed extra costs, in certain parts of the company (Reilly and Williams, 2006).

Keeping the model's integrity

But in solving one problem HR must not create another. Blurring the edges of the model and giving a variety of service options is one thing, but there are also dangers inherent in the partial adoption of the model. The cost and consistency benefits are lost if parts of the organisation can introduce their own payroll, records or intranet systems. If business partners are created and nothing else in the structure changes, the result is likely to be that jobs are merely relabelled, not changed. The embedded HR representative needs a function like a shared service centre to absorb transactional and informational work, or he/she will remain swamped in the day-to-day business of HR management.

There is a different argument with respect to centres of expertise. For small organisations these centres may be an unnecessary indulgence. For larger organisations, the corporate centre may play the role of policy strategist. But in the increasingly sophisticated world of employment, organisations need in some way to deploy deep expertise in areas such as reward, resourcing, OD and learning. Not all of this expertise can be bought in because the organisation has to be able to own its specific policies and strategies.

Finally, two thirds of the survey organisations that had changed their structure did not introduce a shared service centre, including half of those organisations with over 1,000 employees. If these are single-site operations, shared services may be too grand a term for common administrative arrangements, but once an organisation becomes multi-site or multi-divisional, then the cost case for shared services becomes more compelling and the service quality aspects also have to be considered – not least, consistency in delivery. For those operating internationally, the question may have shifted from whether to have shared services, to how many centres there should be and where they should be located.

An international company privately admitted it was struggling with its shared services introduction. This was because it had not properly pushed through the full model, and instead business units had been allowed to keep their own processes, resulting in, for example, seven recruitment processes for the seven business units.

The next evolutionary stage in structure

Some of those who have been involved in HR modernisation for longer than others have now moved on to consider how to improve the model. This may be because of the operational problems caused by segmentation, reported earlier, or due to a perception of the inflexibility of the so called Ulrich form.

One method of dealing with segmentation is to adjust the roles in each of the three legs – eg through adding a case management unit to shared services or by introducing assistant business partners. Another suggestion soon to be made by Ulrich and colleagues is to create a new 'operational executor' leg to the model (Ulrich *et al*, forthcoming).

> '...some practitioners...have wondered whether the "new" structures can accommodate the fast-moving nature of business activity. This seems to be a surprising concern...'

As for the inflexibility of the model, some practitioners in this research have wondered whether the 'new' structures can accommodate the fast-moving nature of business activity. This seems to be a surprising concern and is implicitly rejected by those organisations that have stuck with 'Ulrich' in its purer form. One of the attractions of the model has been precisely that it can be adjusted to changed circumstances (eg new ownership arrangements) – the pieces of Lego can be assembled differently.

A similar concern over 'the inadequacy of structural solutions' in the face of constant change surfaced during the CIPD's change management research (Whittington and Molloy, 2005). The authors' response was that managers needed to acknowledge that 'organisational structures have shorter life-cycles today'.

Is structural change necessary?

A Dublin discussion group participant pushed this point further, arguing that the quality of relationships within HR and between it and the customers were the key to success, not the organisational structure of HR. This is an interesting opinion in the light of the continuing findings that despite structural change, HR managers are still not spending their time on the things that they regard as important – developing HR strategy/policy and contributing to business strategy. Rather, they are still devoting considerable effort to administration and line manager support. Even where the organisational structure has been reformed along 'Ulrich' lines, the time balance within the function is much the same as for those choosing an apparently less radical approach. This bears out the argument of Lawler and Mohrman, cited earlier, that structural reform may not be sufficient to reposition HR.

The question that emerges from this debate is whether structural change is necessary to achieve this objective, even if it is not sufficient. The case-study organisations would say that it is. Nortel, like other companies before it, will be able to show that separating HR transactional work from the transformational will allow those charged with delivering a strategic contribution to shift their workload more in that direction and away from the transactional. The proportion of administrative work should fall, through automation and the use of call centres, and the intranet should allow manager and employee queries to be effectively handled. If HR then fails to become more strategic, the cause of the problem may lie elsewhere – the quality of HR staff, a lack of process reform or the people management capability of line managers. Is it these issues that produce the disappointing figures relating to time spent on deemed-to-be important activities, rather than the inadequacy of structural change?

LEARNING POINTS

❖ Look at your own organisational needs before settling on the organisation of HR. Form should follow function. Take account of:

  ❖ *size*: number of employees

  ❖ *complexity*: dispersed or concentrated workforce, homogeneous or heterogeneous population, common language and common terms and conditions or not

  ❖ *stage of development*: your business priorities

  ❖ *business model*: for example, centralised or decentralised.

❖ In evaluating the options, look at the cost benefits of economies of scale alongside how service quality can be improved.

❖ For those with an existing structure, give particular attention to asking whether it fully satisfies customer needs. If it does not:

  ❖ be prepared to amend it by customising the model to suit different customer groups, but explain the cost implications

  ❖ give managers more operational support through either central casework/delivery teams or through adding to the embedded HR teams.

PROCESSES AND TECHNOLOGY 4

❖ **Process modernisation may be a priority in many organisations and technology can assist in this endeavour.**

❖ **It is not always easy to secure the necessary financial investment even where there are demonstrable savings.**

❖ **Automation of processes has to be carefully undertaken – otherwise, customers will object.**

❖ **Standardisation of processes brings benefits in simplification, use of good practice and benchmarking, but if extended into the policy arena can ill-advisedly impose a single approach on a varied work environment.**

INTRODUCTION

If consolidation through shared services has been one key element in HR transformation, the other elements are standardisation and automation. There appear to be significant practical benefits to automation, such as eliminating routine and repetitive paperwork, streamlining organisational processes and enhancing HR reporting. Overall, it should result in reduced turnaround per transaction, reduced costs per transaction and a decrease in the number of enquiries to HR. Further, e-HR can free up time for HR staff to undertake 'higher value-added' tasks.

Nevertheless, the spread of e-HR and the extent of process improvement vary by sector, organisational size and financial resources. Furthermore, without the proper investment, e-HR may fail to deliver worthwhile savings for HR and quality improvements for customers.

> **'...using automation to free up time does not guarantee that this time will be spent strategically.'**

The CIPD's 2003 survey suggested that many HR professionals believed that time spent on administration was limiting their ability to be more strategic. However, using automation to free up time does not guarantee that this time will be spent strategically.

Moreover, the interviewees from our earlier report felt that the benefits of e-HR had not yet fully delivered, some of them arguing that user needs had been insufficiently recognised. Others felt that e-HR was being used more to transfer HR work to others than to help ease the workload of customers.

Nevertheless, the trend towards e-HR was not questioned by any of these interviewees.

As for standardisation, there is a debate about how far to push it and in what areas of HR work. Are we talking about standard processes or standard policies? And how much does the former depend upon standard technology platforms?

RESEARCH RESULTS

Pressure to improve

To begin with, we tried to establish whether HR's process management and technology were seen as areas in need of improvement. We got feedback through the answers to three questions. In response to the CEO's perception of the quality of HR's performance, HR processes came out as the weakest area in the eyes of HR managers. Nearly 40% of respondents thought that CEOs would not be positive on this item. In a second question, around the same proportion of the survey felt that poor manager and employee self-service capability had adversely affected devolution of people management activities to line management a great deal, and a further 40% felt that it had affected devolution 'a fair amount'. In a third question, nearly a third of respondents identified failed technology as one of the major challenges in HR transformation.

Outsourcing as an option

This would suggest that the technological support that helps underpin HR transformation cannot be taken for granted. The pressure to improve technology and through it to improve processes has led some organisations, such as Centrica, to outsource their shared services operation precisely to fund investment in technology. By contrast, a number of our case-study organisations have been able to fund developments in automation internally as part of their change programme. In two cases (Nortel and Vodafone) the investment in e-HR piggybacked upon investment in finance systems. The business case for the latter was sufficient to get board approval, but HR was able successfully to argue that functional integration was desirable, if not necessary. On its own, the HR case was not seen to be sufficiently strong against competing demands, even if standardisation and automation can lead to demonstrable efficiency gains.

Uptake

What was clear from the case studies was the wide range of levels of automation, relating to differing needs, differing contexts and differing levels of spending. At the more ambitious end of the spectrum is Nortel, as reported in other CIPD research (Parry *et al*, 2007). It introduced manager self-service through the removal of paper-based tools and the transfer of the tasks from HR to line managers, so that the entering and approving of data changes (including those relating to salary) is now done by the line. A small company like Firefly might have more modest ambitions, but nevertheless it felt positive about the quality of its technology and the impact it had, as did the much larger Capita with its self-service system. It had offered benefits in terms of time, efficiency and customer experience. In between, Surrey County Council has addressed the needs of those two thirds of the organisation without computer access by using 'mediated' services, by which a shared service centre operative keys in information on behalf of the employee.

> At Firefly staff can make their holiday bookings or change their personal details on line. The intranet provides comprehensive information – all policies and procedures and job descriptions are held there. All performance and development (eg appraisals/ training) information can be accessed via the intranet too. There is a good back-office HR system, which can explore objectives, development plans, absence levels, leave, all in one place.

Application

Where research participants were more critical was in the detailed application of technology. The HR leader, EMEA (Europe, Middle East and Africa), of Nortel felt, in hindsight, that there should have been more customisation of the vanilla self-service offering, believing that the model they used proved to be insufficiently intuitive. The view from this research participant was that self-service could have been piloted more to establish customer preferences. Complex systems are likely to be problematic where features are

intermittently used and where managers or employees are likely to forget their induction training.

> The former HR director at Hampshire County Council did not feel that HR had sufficient control over the IT solution chosen and that HR did not lead strongly enough on the HR elements of the system. Further, it was felt that the function did not clearly enough articulate its needs or sufficiently consider the end user requirements. The result was that the line did not like the functionality it was offered. The manager desktop was a 'nightmare' – for example, individuals were required to go through five screens to input absence data. However, it was expected that a new version in development will be much more intuitive. The employee desktop was much less contentious. As the then HR director at Hampshire County Council pointed out, the more reliant HR is on technology, the more important it is to have not just systems that work but staff with the skills to operate them properly and to understand why a process is important.

E.ON discovered that process automation can go too far. Its HR services department brought in consultants already working with some of its business customers to look at a number of people management processes. They concluded that the focus of the design was too much on cost and not enough on service, and that some automated processes were unsuitable. In some cases – especially related to sensitive or personal matters – staff were reluctant to use the technology at all. Others did not trust it because they needed the reassurance of speaking to a human being, possibly to confirm that they had done the right thing electronically. The counter-intuitive result was that in these circumstances the automated process cost more time than contacting a call centre. In giving employees that option, HR was offering to manage the complexity rather than foist it onto the customer.

As the Nortel boxed example below shows (and other interviewees and the CIPD's research on technology also indicated), piloting both process changes and new technology is perceived as being worth the effort. Certainly, this need is recognised by Capita in having a policy of piloting 'everything we do' and to engaging customers at an early stage.

> Nortel used a 'conference room pilot' to validate its new global processes. This took place over four days. A variety of global HR staff looked at what had been designed (based on a series of global process workshops and global requirements gathering) and aimed for best practice in finalising what would be the designated global processes. This ensured buy-in, as well as clarifying the right processes to apply.

Process reform

As for process reform itself – which does not necessarily need a technological input, but these days frequently does – again there has been a lot of activity. The boxed example below illustrates what has been done.

Vodafone is improving and standardising processes based on SAP ERP and extensive self-service. This move towards common systems, common processes and a similar operating model is part of an approach to deliver a consistent HR service globally. The advantage from a Vodafone corporate perspective is that management information systems and terminology are the same company-wide. This allows more effective internal benchmarking and comparison to take place, from which the performance of people management can be judged.

Vodafone has a vision of a 'Global HR Process Architecture'. This takes seven work areas (such as learning and development or reward and recognition) and breaks them down into a number of sub-processes. It is then decided whether the process is to be standardised across the Group (such as managing international assignments) or wholly locally designed (such as recognition schemes).

Nortel, similarly, describes its aim as trying to achieve a 'consistent and predictable service, irrespective of geography'. However, it has encountered an unanticipated effect from its process and technological improvement, as set out in the box below.

Managers were able, through manager self-service, to speed up the authorisation part of a task, but the HR processing time remained the same. This meant that the total end-to-end time for process completion was cut, but the proportion consumed by HR rose. Managers became more critical of the slowness of HR, not recognising that processes had overall speeded up.

Similar problems have been experienced by other organisations. Managers can be critical of HR processes because they compare existing performance levels with a past seen through rose-tinted spectacles. Speed of process may not yet be as good as it could be, but may well be better than previously.

Despite the fact that reducing processing time depends to a degree on standardisation, we found that not everybody shares the enthusiasm for commonality. Opponents may be those in operating companies that do not see that the common processes fit their particular circumstances and complain about their inability to change things locally any more.

One response is to accept that the customer base is heterogeneous and to tailor the service to meet particular business unit needs. Thus, at E.ON power stations do not receive the same service in content or delivery (eg in the degree of automation) as the retail organisation. The company accommodates the distinctive business characteristics of its different organisations.

Getting the order right

One question posed in our earlier report on which we sought answers in this phase of the research concerns the order in which change should occur, given that processes, structures, systems and people are all in the mix. Naturally, the answer is complicated because it depends on the starting place. To illustrate:

❖ Nortel is leading with systems change (through the introduction of SAP ERP, specifically the self-service portal), followed by process change, with restructuring last, although all of these changes were deployed as part of the same broader evolution project. However, this is not the first phase of HR transformation. HR shared services was introduced some time before in the largest geographies, and this was therefore the platform to work from.

❖ Vodafone is using an approach of getting the IT system installed and then improving the processes before tackling the people issues.

❖ HMRC is adjusting its HR structure at the same time as e-HR and process re-engineering are launched.

❖ Survey respondents argued for the following sequences:

  ❖ 'Convince the organisation of the need to re-engineer HR processes before identifying the shared services centre solution.'

  ❖ 'The lack of a common IT architecture prevented consolidation' – so install that first.

> **'Whether in practice technological change, process and structural reform are distinct from each other is a question that needs further exploration.'**

Whether in practice technological change, process and structural reform are distinct from each other is a question that needs further exploration. In some organisations change feels like 'permanent revolution' because the structure is constantly evolving, along with the expansion of manager and employee self-service and process improvement. At any one time, one element might have more attention than the others, but there is such a symbiotic relationship between structure, technology and process that they all move forward together.

Thus, Nortel can cut out the role of HR advisers in part because of self-service because historically much of the time of the advisers was taken up with handling paper authorisations. The latter are now more automated in the context of simpler decision-making procedures.

For those companies that have outsourced their HR administration, the change sequence has been clearer. The pulling together of transactional activities into shared services has facilitated outsourcing. This has led some HR staff, especially in the public sector, to fear that the introduction of shared services is the precursor to outsourcing.

IMPLICATIONS

The story of automation and standardisation is not unlike that of consolidation. They are regarded by most organisations as necessary for both efficiency and effectiveness reasons, and in the case of process reform in order to respond to customer challenge. Yet the devil is in the detail of the design decisions made and how these are implemented.

The need to sell the message

It is not perhaps surprising given the results of other CIPD research (Parry *et al*, 2007) to report the difficulties of organisations in getting funding for e-HR, even where the return on investment is clear. Parry *et al* talked about how problematic it was to put together the business case for investment in technology in HR compared with other functions. It appeared from some of our discussions that investment in HR is not felt to be as business-critical as Finance, despite the prospect of a good return on investment, evidenced by results such as cost saving, faster cycle times, giving greater control over data to managers and employees, and better management information.

E-HR can deliver these real benefits, but if badly introduced can irritate users. Some of the early adopters of e-HR found resistance from managers to standardisation because the technology demanded simple processes and even common policies. This did not make sense in multi-site companies with wide variation in business activity. The Nortel advice to select systems with a premium on intuitiveness or to customise if necessary seems sensible. If managers in particular are told they are being empowered by HR and then presented with substandard technology, they might revolt. The resistance may not be overt, but may come from drowning HR in queries or in hiring clerks themselves to tackle the e-enabled administrative burden. The E.ON case study also illustrates the limitations of automation. It should not be pursued for its own sake, but

because it delivers an organisational good – cost reduction, quality improvement, refocusing of activity – all of which may require some selling to the line.

Standardisation offers benefits

It is hard to see, however, how process reform will not be tied up with some degree of standardisation. There is a long-standing ambition of HR to simplify processes and choose best practice solutions. This will mean imposing a common approach to processes such as recruitment or training. However, it is perhaps necessary to draw a number of distinctions in the standardisation debate. There is the standardisation of:

❖ *the IT platform or tools* – Some organisations are prescriptive in requiring all operating companies to operate with the same HRIS and payroll, and to use a common intranet. It allows better knowledge-sharing, offers joint funding and avoids duplicating costs.

❖ *processes and procedures: how activities are performed* – This could range from the way new hires are inducted to standard offer letters. It permits organisations to operate to quality standards across business units and to apply universal good practice. It means that moving staff in and out of roles is easier if there are set procedures to follow than where they are subject to the idiosyncrasies of an individual process owner. Standardisation is less contentious in a UK context than in a global environment. In the former situation, operating environments may not differ as much as in the latter. Organisations are likely to argue for common processes, not least because using common processes allows shared procurement of training or recruitment services that offers a major cost saving.

> '**Standardisation is less contentious in a UK context than in a global environment.**'

❖ *policies: the rules governing activities* – This is much more debatable and harder to specify because in some companies policies are seen as processes. Thus, a common performance management approach could be seen as a process or a policy. Clearly some policies are so location-specific that they would not be standardised. For others there is a tension between corporate desire to do things in the same way and the local wish to reflect local cultural preferences or customs.

Some organisations carefully consider standardisation from this muti-dimensional perspective. The cost and consistency argument is more persuasive for a common IT platform than for processes and policies, although the latter are not all of a piece. Neil Roden (HR director of RBS) has cautioned that companies need to be careful with standardisation, respectful of culture, history and context, especially where individual operating companies may reflect independently successful brands (Reilly and Williams, 2006). Some companies, like Shell, have a long track record of integration of the fundamentals of HR policy and practice. Others – for example, Siemens – on their performance management system may demand commonality in particular areas. The Vodafone example, albeit against a global background, shows how organisations can systematically review their policies and practices to see where the benefits of commonality outweigh the drawbacks. Sharing a recruitment process can bring major procurement savings. Having the same international deployment mechanisms may be essential to deliver consistent treatment to expatriates, whereas having a common approach to local remuneration or employee relations flies in the face of different labour markets and employment regulations.

In the context of the changing nature of HR, process simplification and standardisation affects the role of HR. As we described earlier, through exiting from some processes and streamlining others, HR is able to concentrate on those tasks which cannot easily be automated or transferred to other owners. As the Lawler *et al* research (2003) shows, though, automation of processes may release time – but that has to be used productively, which remains a real challenge for the function.

LEARNING POINTS

❖ Undertake a process mapping exercise to understand how efficient and effective your processes are.

❖ Automate, not for its own sake but where there are quality and efficiency benefits – and take careful note of customer requirements both in the choice of processes to automate and in the way in which they are automated. Especially automate only 'low-touch' processes.

❖ Similarly, standardise where there are gains in accuracy, simplicity, cost or good practice – but once more do not insist on commonality unless it is really necessary.

❖ Be especially careful when transferring work to managers. Manage expectations, adopt a low-key more-action-than-talk approach and ensure that the processes are easy to operate.

OUTSOURCING

5

✛ **Outsourcing remains a tactical rather than strategic matter for most organisations.**

✛ **Outsourcing is limited in scope, mainly to specific activities where specialist skills are available.**

✛ **Some global companies are exploring offshoring, but in a tentative manner.**

✛ **There are examples of other approaches – insourcing, cross-functional sharing and strategic partnerships.**

INTRODUCTION

The question of who delivers HR services has perhaps been more contentious, and received more air time in recent years than how these services are delivered. Organisations have considered whether to keep service delivery in-house or whether it is better to use external providers. A number of high-profile shared service centre deals have left some practitioners with the impression that the introduction of shared services will lead to outsourcing, and it would appear that consolidating transactional activities and isolating them in a shared service centre will make spin-off easier.

Nevertheless, our earlier report suggested that this subject is over-hyped. HR shared services might be ripe for outsourcing according to the suppliers, but the figures suggest a more limited market. Organisations routinely externalise service delivery for a number of activities, where there is a better price to be obtained or specialist skills can be called upon. However, it would appear that this is not a growing trend. Nor is it true that, apart from a number of high profile deals, there is extensive whole-service outsourcing. A 2003 CIPD survey of HR practitioners (CIPD, 2003) concluded that the outsourcing market was broadly static, some organisations increasing their use of external providers and others cutting back. The main growth areas were training and development, recruitment and employee counselling.

Furthermore, WERS (the Workplace Employee Relations Survey) 2004 suggests that outsourcing is specific to certain activities and limited in extent – training, payroll and resourcing of temporary positions were most commonly outsourced.

The main reasons for outsourcing include cutting costs, improving the quality of service, and allowing organisations to concentrate on their core business. However, in terms of whether these goals have been achieved, the picture is less clear. There appears to be some evidence that outsourcing has resulted in cost reductions, but little evidence that organisations have been able to concentrate on higher-value activities or to become more strategic as a result of outsourcing.

Nevertheless, not only suppliers continue to believe that organisations will increasingly outsource. Ulrich, for example, believes that the larger firms will increasingly outsource bundles of HR transactions, while smaller firms will probably outsource discrete practices (Ulrich and Brockbank, 2005). This may be a US view of the outsourcing market. Certainly, within the UK some blue-chip companies have contracted out significant chunks of HR activity. However, there are those that prefer to keep an integrated service largely in-house, perhaps for fear that the service segmentation of the three-legged stool structure becomes fragmentation with outsourcing – where day-to-day operations are split from strategy and policy direction, and undertaken by different companies. There have indeed been examples of outsourcing not having worked, resulting in the renegotiation of deals or the bringing operations back in-house.

> **'...offshoring of HR activities seems to be largely limited to transactional processing rather than to include the whole range of a shared service centre workload.'**

Offshoring may compound these problems if HR activities are even more geographically dispersed. Of course, offshoring is not always distant outsourcing. Organisations may offshore activities to wholly-owned subsidiaries remote from operational centres or use a low-cost operational centre for certain types of HR work. Thus far, offshoring of HR activities seems to be largely limited to transactional processing rather than to include the whole range of a shared service centre workload. HR call centres are much less often to be found offshore than are, for example, retail call centres.

RESEARCH RESULTS

The incidence of outsourcing

This picture of limited outsourcing is confirmed by our survey, in which only 4% of respondents with an HR shared services operation said that they wholly outsourced it. Around a quarter outsourced part of their shared services activities. The vast majority of organisations maintain their shared services operation in-house.

Selective outsourcing was also practised by all our case-study organisations. For example, pensions administration, payroll, flexible benefits administration, training delivery and insurance are all outsourced at Ernst & Young. Surrey County Council used third parties to deliver training and to operate shared services for part of its organisation. Firefly just outsources payroll and the provision of some benefits.

Future prospects

Looking ahead, 11% of the survey participants expect HR shared services to be outsourced in three years, and half expect to partly outsource some of their shared services outsourcing. The fact that only one in ten of organisations seems likely to fully outsource suggests that business process outsourcing (BPO) will remain a small fraction of the available outsourcing market, especially when intention-to-outsource responses tend to exaggerate the actual outcome.

When talking to individual organisations about the future, caution with respect to outsourcing generally came through. There are those – like the HR director at Surrey County Council – who are positive about the benefits and would reduce HR to its core. By contrast, the former HR director at Hampshire County Council felt that there was 'no appetite' for outsourcing because of scepticism over the long-term benefits and the degree to which it takes skills out of the function. The MOD took the view that they wanted to keep their shared services operation in-house so that HR would be better able to influence the business and to ensure maximum efficiency gains for the Department. Then there are those who argue that if an organisation is efficient in the way it sets up its shared services operation, including process design, then there is little cost for a supplier to remove. The economics then become questionable: how can the supplier be cost-competitive and still make a profit? If, conversely, an organisation passes a mess of unreformed processes to the supplier, it will suffer the financial consequences.

Moreover, there is the potential inflexibility of outsourcing to consider. Nortel entered into a long-term contract in a business environment that had thereafter changed radically. It became a smaller company, but the outsourcing contract was based on volumes of activity that had become out of date. Nortel therefore chose to bring administrative services back in-house to regain control over its costs.

> Cable and Wireless had a very similar story to Nortel, in that the business changed radically after the outsourcing deal was struck but the pricing was significantly influenced by volume assumptions. As volumes fell, the price per transaction increased. However, there was also a change of management philosophy affected by the alteration in the commercial environment. After the telecoms bubble burst, the injunction was to make all costs variable. Outsourcing chunks of HR was a logical consequence. The challenges of the outsourcing approach became apparent, especially the loss of tacit knowledge, and the business needs altered with the acquisition of Energis in the UK.

Despite the sort of reservations expressed above, we know that some organisations will still outsource. This may be for reasons of focus (concentrating on the high-value-added activities) as much as to do with cost. As we saw in Chapter 4 (and Centrica is a case in point) organisations may want to upgrade their technology, but unlike Nortel and Vodafone, cannot secure the necessary funds. This inclines them towards outsourcing as the best (or only) solution.

Alternatives to outsourcing

There are, however, alternatives to outsourcing. Three of our other case-study organisations – Capita, Surrey County Council and the MOD – insourced some of their shared services operations (ie transferred work to another part of their organisation). Capita naturally did this because it used the service operation it offers to external clients. The shared services centre delivers HR administration, payroll and first line support on rules-based queries to managers. Capita's other 'centres of excellence' provide occupational health, pensions, recruitment and outplacement services. The company takes payroll, records, occupational health, pensions and outplacement services from its commercial shared service centre.

Surrey County Council removed all non-professional tasks to its shared service centres. One is fully outsourced; the other – dealing with 13,000 of its 33,000 employees – is part of a cross-functional centre in Corporate Services. The payroll/records section is quite well integrated, but stands apart from the separate Procurement Finance and IT units. There is some sharing at peak workloads, but not yet full resourcing flexibility. The MOD created the 'People, Pay and Pensions Agency' to undertake its shared services work. See the description in the box below.

> The MOD's People, Pay and Pensions Agency (PPPA) employs 1,100 staff at three main UK sites. Full implementation will occur in April 2008, after a three-year transition. When finalised it will offer 'an integrated set of simplified, standardised HR services to MOD employees and their line managers'. The Agency is expected to handle in excess of 1 million calls per year and deal with in excess of 5,000 items of correspondence (faxes, letters and emails) per month.

For public sector organisations in particular there are opportunities to achieve economies of scale through cross-organisational sharing. Hampshire County Council is exploring this by considering teaming up with district councils within the County on sharing administrative effort. The Council is planning its own shared service centre and could include other organisations' transactional work within its remit. There are some mature examples in the NHS and local government of sharing resources, and discussions are under way at central government level. The MOD's People, Pay and Pensions services are, for example, offered to non-MOD customers, such as the Charity Commission which receives a pensions service from the PPPA. There are fewer cases in the private sector of companies having shared HR services – there are obvious commercial objections.

Another approach is that of strategic partnership. Here, organisations link with specialist organisations to undertake some of their work because it is either too complex to be undertaken internally or would require too great an investment in skills. Fujitsu, for example, has a strategic partnership with Watson Wyatt to carry out its pensions work.

Offshoring

> '...there is...a debate about the merits of offshoring provision outside of the UK.'

Although some organisations seek to outsource either all or parts of their shared service provision to other providers, there is also a debate about the merits of offshoring provision outside of the UK. The argument about offshoring must simply be about cost: to take account of the so-called wage arbitrage (ie the differential between sender and receiver of work) and perhaps cheaper accommodation. There is a difference between those organisations that are choosing to locate work at one of their own lower-cost locations within the company and those that outsource to an external provider offshore.

Building your own shared service centre abroad is a half-way house between these positions.

Vodafone is carefully dipping its toe in the offshore arena by passing over to an East European global shared service centre a limited range of administrative tasks, such as maintaining position data and verifying global data integrity. Whether further activities will be transferred later will not be decided until there is experience of how well it works.

Nortel's situation illustrates the problem faced by a number of global companies. It has four shared service centres (in the USA, the UK, France and Hong Kong) delivering transactional services across the world. Wage rates are of course high in some of these locations, but they are home to significant employee populations. Moreover, it is evident to Nortel that it is easier to deliver services to your home than to a foreign community. Errors are more common when processing tasks that are dealt with in an unfamiliar way. For example, in the case of employment contracts, what requires a reissue of contract in the USA is different from the UK. This means that American administrative staff have to learn to be familiar with UK custom and practice, which takes time and money. Another organisation also pointed to the improvement in the quality of customer experience through collocating all the shared service centre elements – call centre, both first and second escalation levels, and processing. This is due to fewer handoffs and better cross-organisational learning.

IMPLICATIONS

If it is true that the 'noise' about outsourcing is quite out of line with the actual or potential market, it vindicates those who believe outsourcing is a distraction to the question of how to deliver HR services and that it is a tactical, not a strategic, matter.

> 'For smaller organisations, third-party providers may offer a size of operation that delivers real economies...'

But to those engaged in outsourcing, this must seem a strange conclusion to draw. These organisations must see benefits to outsourcing. It may be tempting to outsource a service which is not delivering well or which the organisation is finding difficult to manage. Nevertheless, if you take the view that you should not outsource a problem, then organisations will only be considering activities in reasonable shape. If the supplier has to make a profit, then indeed it is hard to see where the supplier makes a surplus. The answer may lie with scale or technology. For smaller organisations, third-party providers may offer a size of operation that delivers real economies and, as we described in Chapter 4, quality technology is not open to some organisations. The customer benefit may possibly lie both in the provision of technology and in saving the difficulty of in-house implementation. This gives a competitive advantage to technology-based suppliers. Therefore, the pattern of outsourcing may remain concentrated on specific services where organisations do not have the expertise (eg employee counselling) or where there is a scale advantage in externalisation. The bigger outsourcing deals will be seen either to fund e-enablement when internal funds are denied or where HR is treated as marginal to the success of the enterprise.

Offshoring is in many ways more of a distraction: it is really only outsourcing or insourcing, but to a distant location, and, according to CIPD research, it is not even that common for HR activities. The offshoring of HR services is still relatively uncommon. For example, in a recent CIPD survey, only 7% of respondents had either offshored or were considering offshoring HR activities (CIPD, 2006b). If the activity is offshored through an outsourcing deal, the same points made above apply. If it is the relocation of work within the organisation, how does this differ from transferring work to regional centres? The only difference is that the HR administrative work is not located close to the large employee populations (such as the UK) but to low-cost locations. The challenge here is similar to the creation of shared service centres in the first place: dispersion of activity makes knowledge-sharing and service to the customer harder. This does not mean that it cannot be done, but the organisation should acknowledge that for some expense reduction it may suffer in terms of reduced service quality.

LEARNING POINTS

❖ Organisations should be careful to avoid jumping on what might incorrectly be perceived to be the outsourcing bandwagon. They should never outsource problems and should be mindful that suppliers have to make a profit. The conclusion to draw is that outsourcing only makes sense in process outsourcing where there are scale or technology benefits. Contracting out specialist tasks has the different logic of obtaining access to expertise.

❖ Organisations should take care to ensure that their outsourcing contracts are sufficiently flexible to deal with organisational change.

❖ Offshoring is best considered for process transactions rather than for call centres and again is likely to be driven by cost considerations.

ROLES

6

❖ **Defining new roles is a significant challenge in HR transformation.**

❖ **There are different conceptions of the business partner role, the most important of which is whether the business partner is accountable for the whole service.**

❖ **Although there was a positive appreciation of the work of business partners, there were a number of criticisms made relating to their competence and relationships with others.**

❖ **There are centres of expertise in a number of HR subject areas, most commonly for learning and development.**

INTRODUCTION

We described the role of HR in the chapter on the purpose of HR (Chapter 2) . Here, we examine the specific roles – ie types of job – within HR. This overlaps with the structural changes to the function we covered in Chapter 3. Whereas we considered there the overall structure of HR, the survey and, in particular, the case studies offered insights into the specific roles that form part of the three-legged stool. The key roles/jobs we cover here are introduced below.

Business partners

There has been a significant increase in demand for business partners, with the CIPD's research showing that the business partner has become the most attractive role for HR practitioners (CIPD, 2003). Previous CIPD work (Tamkin *et al*, 2006) suggested that many organisations were finding it difficult to obtain people of the right calibre for business partner roles. The views of the experts IES interviewed for its first CIPD report varied, but were generally cautious and many did not like the concept for various reasons, including the implication that it suggests a division between strategic contribution and transactional work.

One expert cited three problems with the business partner role:

❖ that it was insufficiently defined

❖ that it did not take enough account of customer wishes

❖ that there were not enough HR people with the skills and credibility to perform the role.

Subject expert

The introduction of centres of expertise relates to the need for deep expertise in key HR areas. In the three-legged stool they can offer their expertise to the generalist business partners and, in some cases, directly to managers, and they can act as the next level of escalation up from call centres. In some models the emphasis is on policy development; in others they play more of an internal consultancy role. Centres of expertise have been challenged as either too divorced from operational life to offer tailored advice or insufficiently aware of external good practice. Experts are therefore vulnerable to replacement by external consultants, and their work is vulnerable to being absorbed by other parts of the HR structure.

Administrator

As described by Ulrich (1997), the administrative expert role seems to be the poor relation in the HR functional family. This is because HR wishes to move up the so-called 'value chain', reducing the amount of transactional activity and increasing the added-value component that is seen to come from a strategic contribution. Cutting administration is thus perceived as a good thing and something towards which organisations strive. However, line managers appear to value this role highly and various commentators point out that failure to perform administrative tasks can limit access to 'higher-value' work, in addition to creating difficulties in its own right.

> '...the administrative expert role seems to be the poor relation in the HR functional family.'

Besides being relegated in the eyes of some practitioners to a structural backwater of shared services, automation has also eroded the input that administrative staff can make. Ulrich claims that process re-engineering and e-HR have resulted in HR reducing the resources it dedicates to administrative work from 70–80% to 15–20% without loss of quality (Ulrich and Brockbank, 2005). Another study by Mercer in 2003 (quoted in CIPD, 2006a) reported that 25% of time is spent on transactions and record-keeping, but the study added that organisations wanted to cut it back further to 11% of desired time.

It is difficult for organisations to succeed in cutting administrative activity (and the associated jobs) through standardisation, consolidation and automation while at the same time arguing the importance of these roles and maintaining the morale of incumbents. This position is further complicated by the clamour to outsource these non-core tasks, especially in light of the difficulty of defining where administration begins and ends.

RESEARCH RESULTS

Defining roles was the most frequently selected challenge in restructuring HR given in our survey of HR managers, some 42% of respondents identifying with this problem. This suggests that there is still a big jump between the theory of the model and its practical implementation. Case-study organisations illustrated this by way of example, as described below.

BUSINESS PARTNERS

Scope

Apart from Firefly, all our case-study organisations had business partners in place, although the scope or focus of the role varied across the organisations. Capita suggests that 'business partners offer a professional advisory and support role'. Hampshire County Council sees business partners' role as to act as a 'conduit' between the line and the centre. The view here is that they should understand the business and drive changes at the corporate centre to reflect business units' needs. Consultancy skills are important at Reuters, because they 'diagnose, scope and frame' projects.

These differences may be more of emphasis in what skills are thought to be important. A bigger question is the relationship between the business partner and the function as a whole. At Vodafone, business partners are accountable for the whole HR service. They encourage managers' employee engagement responsibilities, they develop capability through their resourcing actions, and they plan ahead, looking for future skills gaps. Similarly, Reuters' business partners scope the service requirements for their business unit and agree the HR SLAs with business customers, not just to cover their own work but also that of the shared services operation. This means that if there are systems problems, it is the business partner who is expected to sort them out.

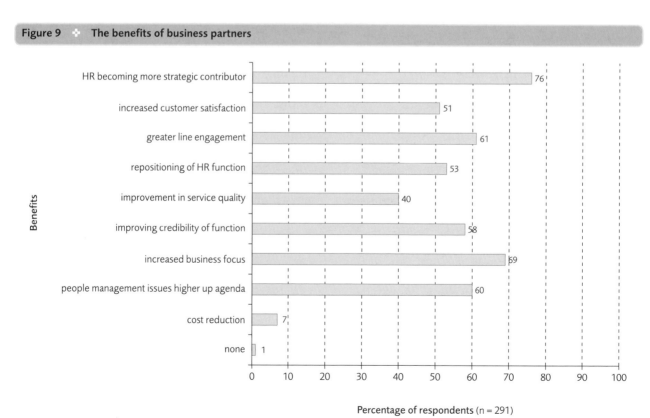

Figure 9   The benefits of business partners

Source: CIPD survey (2007)

At other organisations – like Capita and the MOD – business partners are not accountable for the HR service, only for their own contribution.

Contribution

Overall, there was a generally positive assessment of the contribution of the business partner. The benefits of business partners according to the survey were reported earlier and are set out in Figure 9 on page 34. This shows that for a majority of organisations the introduction of business partners has helped HR meet the principal aims of its transformation – namely, to become a more strategic contributor and to achieve greater engagement with managers through an increased business focus. The fact that the proportion of time HR is spending on strategic issues has gone up provides contributory evidence to the progress being made.

The case-study organisations illustrated these points. The HR manager at Hampshire County Council remarked that business partners were now leading corporate projects in a way that would not have happened before. 'HR used to come in at the end and pick up HR issues.' Now the function is 'driving strategic projects'. At Ernst & Young there appeared to be more confidence from managers in the business partners' ability to tackle strategic issues. They are now wanted at 'partner' meetings.

Nevertheless, there were still challenges in the implementation of the business partner role that need to be faced. These were some points made by case-study interviewees, who, in some cases, are still in the throes of change:

❖ 'Business partners do not know which camp they sit in.' This observation concerns the question whether business partners are agents of corporate HR sitting in the business or agents of the business unit trying to influence the centre. It is closely related to the fear that business partners will go 'native'. This in fact happened in the early days at Hampshire County Council before they understood that they were the 'lynchpins' in making the model work. The view in this organisation's HR team is that business partners cannot get too close to their business colleagues because they need some 'distance' to protect corporate interests.

❖ 'Business partners promise the earth because they leave someone else to deliver.' This illustrates one of the risks of segmented services. The business partners may commission projects or tasks, but they are not involved in implementation. Where there are delivery units or consultants in centres of expertise, they execute the plans. There has been particular criticism of ill-informed learning and development initiatives being launched because business partners are frequently weak in this area.

❖ 'Business partners end up doing operational work because line managers ask them, not the centres of expertise.' This

is another potential consequence of the new model. Managers are more likely to go to their business partner than to distant centres of expertise or a shared service centre. Some organisations are encouraging business partners to be ruthless in redirecting managers elsewhere.

❖ 'Business partners are still held accountable for poor delivery although it's the shared service centre providing the work.' This is another case of the allocation of responsibility either not being clear or not being accepted. As we have seen, in some organisations business partners are explicitly accountable for the whole service provision. In others, they are not (teams are accountable for their own actions) but nonetheless get drawn into the work of others. As one respondent claimed, where the shared service team is 'not up to speed yet', the business partners get dragged into transactional activity, leading to a 'duplication' of tasks.

❖ 'Business partners need to get out more.' This refers to a skills or dispositional question. It has echoes of Richie Furlong's (ex-Unilever and Cabinet Office) question whether business partners are 'up for it, as well as up to it' (Reilly and Williams, 2006). Business partners cannot be effective if they are not engaging with business executives, seeking out what good practice is to be found elsewhere or finding out what the competition is doing. One view expressed was that their business partners were too introspective and not leading the organisation sufficiently, but following others too much.

> 'Business partners cannot be effective if they are not engaging with business executives, seeking out what good practice is to be found elsewhere or finding out what the competition is doing.'

❖ 'Business partners are expected to do it all and can't.' This problem occurs when managers still want to use a one-stop-shop approach and contact business partners rather than ring a call centre or approach a service centre. Business partners have to be both clear as to their role and tough at redirecting managers, but great care must be taken to avoid irritating customers.

❖ 'Managers do not understand the role that business partners can play.' This may not be a rejection of the concept by managers – rather, they may be simply unused to HR offering to make a strategic contribution. In the particular example given, managers did not realise the 'help' that was available with business plans. This might indeed be business partners responding successfully to a need, but it could also be a case of educating managers about the importance of people management in their plans and strategies.

Figure 10 ❖ Problems with business partners

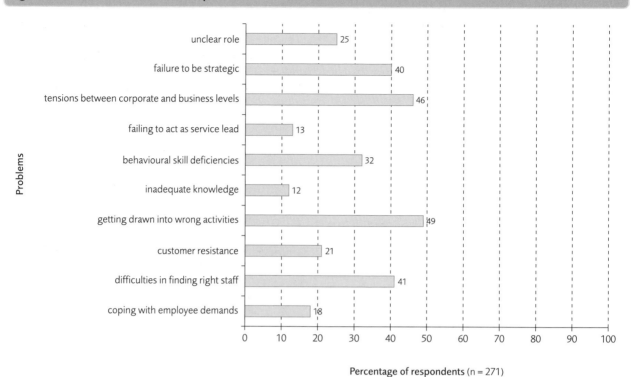

Source: CIPD survey (2007)

The extent of these challenges prompted one HR director to suggest that business partners were the least valuable part of the team, and if cuts had to be made, it was in this area that they would fall. He criticised business partners as 'interfering do-gooders', not strategic contributors.

His viewpoint was in the minority. Those interviewees who were positive about their business partners were perhaps less vocal in their description of progress, but it does appear that other organisations have to work hard to achieve a successful outcome.

Some of these points resonate with the survey results, shown in Figure 10 above – ie, the failure to be strategic, tensions with the corporate centre, and the risk of going 'native' .

Resourcing

Sourcing of the business partners has previously been reported as difficult (Tamkin *et al*, 2006) and the above remarks suggest it still is. Indeed, 41% of survey respondents, as shown in Figure 10, identified this as a problem with the business partner role, and a third had concerns about their skills.

From the case-study interviews, Capita reported that although they did not have major problems resourcing the role, sourcing them from a wide background, there was an issue at times in getting the right quality of applicants. As a consequence of the market situation, salaries have gone up for these roles.

Hampshire County Council had successfully brought in staff from the private sector (eg banking) and they had a beneficial effect in terms of coaching and developing others. The former HR director remarked that skill investment in these external recruits that had already been made was significant – much more than could be provided by an organisation such as theirs.

In another organisation it was felt by HR interviewees that the new structure had benefits for business partners in terms of satisfaction and challenge that had led to a lower resignation rate.

> 'Some of those who took the [business partner] role needed to make a major shift in mind-set, which was not straightforward.'

This last remark indicates that there was some support for concerns about skills in our case studies. More than one organisation thought that at least initially the quality in the business partner population was uneven, especially in their capability to be strategic – to the extent that one organisation worried that their 'mediocrity' made it hard to sustain their cost. Some of those who took the role needed to make a major shift in mind-set, which was not straightforward. One line manager commented that 'the quality varies from superb to one wonders how they managed to find their way to work!'

Unlike in the CIPD careers research (Tamkin *et al*, 2006), there was not so much discussion on the merits or otherwise of bringing in managers from the line to perform business partner roles. There are those who agree with Ulrich that this is a positive move in that there is a transfer of skills/knowledge (both ways) but also it shows the indivisible nature of people management or, at least, that it is a shared activity. The contrary view is that it denies opportunities for development for HR staff, since the traffic is nearly all one-way.

CENTRES OF EXPERTISE

Scope

Having described the advantages and disadvantages of the centres of expertise concept earlier, here we consider how these units are best established. In the case studies there was some combination in their role of the following:

❖ policy formulation

❖ execution of policy change

❖ advice to business partners and sometimes directly to managers

❖ an escalation point for the call centre to receive difficult queries.

Which combination applied depended heavily on the remits of the other parts of HR – eg the role of the corporate centre in policy-making, how the shared service centre was set up. For example, Surrey County Council develops HR policies separately from its subject-matter experts. The latter concentrate on procedural issues. Hampshire County Council has administrative functions combined with expertise in its centres of expertise.

Where there are not experts at hand, our organisations seem to use lawyers more than consultants. This may reflect the fact that good risk management in employment law requires specialist advice, whereas policy development can be done more easily (and effectively) in-house. The use of external help in place of internal experts was not otherwise discussed.

As to content areas covered by the centres of expertise, Figure 11 shows the survey responses. Of the 229 organisations in our survey that were using centres of expertise, the most common centre dealt with training/learning and development – 79% of respondents had a centre of excellence for this area.

Centres of expertise are also common for reward and resourcing areas. These particular centres were seen in roughly two thirds of those with this structure. Just over half had an employee relations centre of expertise, and just under half have an OD expertise unit.

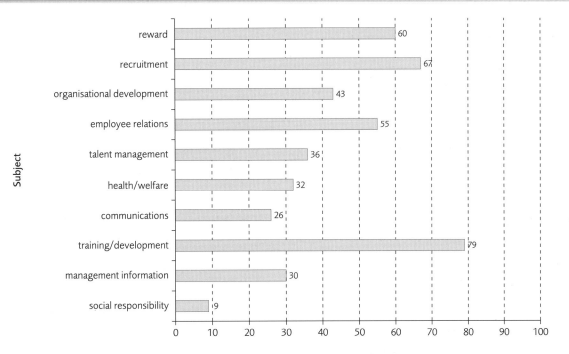

Figure 11 ❖ Work areas with their own centre of expertise

Source: CIPD survey (2007)

Percentage of respondents (n = 229)

reward — 60
recruitment — 67
organisational development — 43
employee relations — 55
talent management — 36
health/welfare — 32
communications — 26
training/development — 79
management information — 30
social responsibility — 9

Figure 12 ❖ **Benefits of centres of expertise**

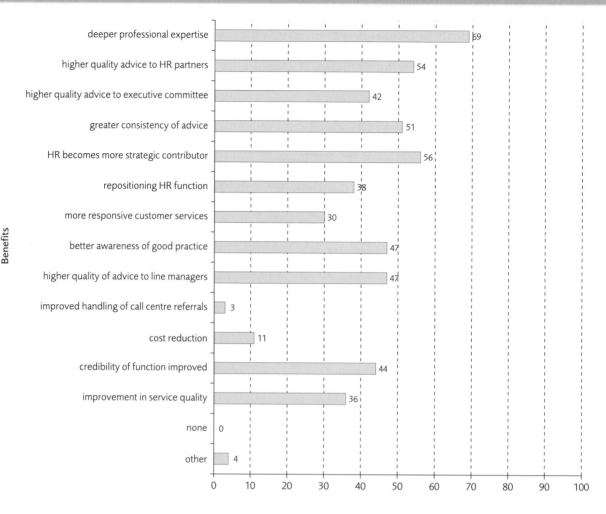

Benefits

- deeper professional expertise — 69
- higher quality advice to HR partners — 54
- higher quality advice to executive committee — 42
- greater consistency of advice — 51
- HR becomes more strategic contributor — 56
- repositioning HR function — 38
- more responsive customer services — 30
- better awareness of good practice — 47
- higher quality of advice to line managers — 47
- improved handling of call centre referrals — 3
- cost reduction — 11
- credibility of function improved — 44
- improvement in service quality — 36
- none — 0
- other — 4

Percentage of respondents (n = 227)

Source: CIPD survey (2007)

Reuters has five centres of 'excellence' in:

❖ organisation development

❖ learning and development

❖ remuneration and international assignments

❖ HR controls and compliance

❖ HR information and transformation.

Much less common are centres of expertise for what might be regarded as the peripheral aspects of HR – health and safety, management information, CSR and communications. Despite its current status as a vital concept, talent management has a centre of expertise in only around a third of organisations in this survey.

Whether OD and learning and development are seen to be part of HR or independent functions is an important matter in some organisations (eg the MOD) or sectors (eg health) where there has been a tendency to separate out the various roles that have a large people management component. The MOD has 'skill champions' in the context of an organisation without centres of expertise. Skills champions (who are senior managers within the line) provide the personnel director with a functional, strategic overview of business critical issues within their job family that informs the development of critical skills areas across the MOD. This distinguishes them from business partners who focus on issues down through a business area.

NHS Trusts sometimes have OD and workforce planning specialists who are separate from HR. These

Figure 13 ❖ **Problems with centres of expertise**

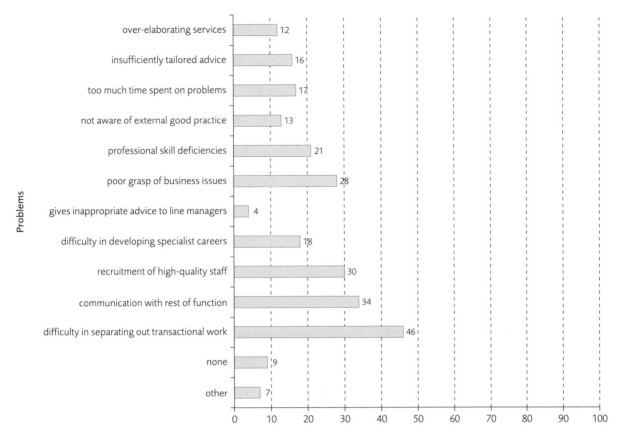

Source: CIPD survey (2007)

arrangements create further interfaces to manage beyond those created by having a three-legged stool model of service delivery.

Benefits

The introduction (or role refinement) of experts has largely benefited organisations through the quality of their expertise, the advice they give and the strategic benefits that result. The better awareness of 'good practice' for nearly half the respondents probably helped in this regard.

Figure 12, opposite, shows the survey responses.

Challenges

We set out in Chapter 3 the problems with centres of expertise that relate to the overall structural change – separating out transactional work, communication with the result of the function – that were the leading problems, according to the

survey. Some of the other problems identified by research were not so prevalent in our study (see Figure 13, above). For example, less than a fifth of respondents selected 'over-elaborating' services, spending too much time on problems, being insufficiently aware of external practice or insufficiently tailoring advice to business need, although closer to a third identified a poor grasp of business issues.

However, there were some negative messages from case-study participants. One embedded HR manager complained that centres of expertise appeared remote even if they were only 10 miles away. He commented that they 'might as well have been on the other side of the moon'. Perhaps to counter this impression, Ernst & Young uses account managers within the centres of expertise who are the single point of contact with the business customers, and it is their role to communicate. The firm also works hard on knowledge-sharing elsewhere. The centres of expertise have regular meetings with the HR shared service centre – regular operational meetings and quarterly strategy meetings. Policy implementation is discussed at these meetings, and parties are convinced it improves implementation.

As with business partners, the challenges that HR directors have with centres of expertise include resourcing difficulties.

As Figure 13 shows, nearly a third of organisations reported recruitment difficulties and a fifth skill deficiencies. These results bear out the evidence from the CIPD's research on HR careers (Tamkin *et al*, 2006) that organisations find it hard to get good-quality staff in reward and OD especially.

SHARED SERVICES

Scope

The principal goal of the new model of HR operations is to separate out 'thinking from doing' with transactional tasks included in shared service centres. Vodafone's global shared service centre is described as being 'responsible for the execution of common, standardised, transactional HR activity which cannot be achieved through automation alone'.

Payroll may be part of an HR shared service centre, undertaken by Finance or outsourced. Call centres may be in use, and they may or may not be part of the shared services operation. Vodafone's UK call centre, 'AskHR', is part of its shared services concept. It deals with a range of employee as well as manager queries with an escalation to experts where necessary. Other organisations locate it separately, as in the 'Information Bureau' at Surrey County Council, although the separation from shared services is probably because the latter is located in a different – Corporate Services – department. The Information Bureau is staffed by non-HR people and is expected to handle 80% of the phone calls. This may include in many cases referring people back to information on the intranet. The HR 'duty desk' acts as the second level up in call centre escalation, referring to the case-work section the 20% of calls classed as 'difficult'.

> HMRC's HR shared services deals with 'first line' queries from managers and employees. It is linked to the learning enquiry service. It administers online facilities, such as leave applications and travel expenses. It is responsible for the HR part of the organisation's intranet. Records administration is done by shared services. There is some payroll facility, complicated by the different ways the Inland Revenue and HM Customs and Excise dealt with payroll.

Pros and cons

As to the benefits of introducing shared services, Table 2 gives more detail on the survey results reported earlier. Offsetting the positive messages on service, customer satisfaction and HR's repositioning as more strategic and credible, are concerns that cost reduction seems to have been more modest and HR staff less satisfied with change than one would hope.

As to the case studies, Vodafone is positive about the benefits its AskHR call centre brings. Much of the content concerns what might be called employee relations issues. The quality of service, especially in case management, is better than before. Employees feel they get the sort of personal response they could not get through HR managers in the past, not least because the HR managers were difficult to contact. HMRC reports resource savings, faster service and more consistent advice. It was acknowledged, though, that it takes time for these quality improvements to come through, partly to allow the technology to mature and partly for service centre staff to

Table 2 ❖ The benefits of shared services				
	No change (%)	Some change (%)	Major change (%)	Total
cost reduction	27	60	13	100%
improvement in service quality	14	57	29	100%
more responsive customer service	21	49	30	100%
more commercial approach to HR	24	52	25	100%
improving credibility of function	25	45	31	100%
repositioning HR	18	48	34	100%
HR more strategic	19	50	31	100%
more satisfied HR staff	38	45	17	100%
HR time shifted to value-added services	16	59	25	100%

Source: CIPD survey (2007)

Figure 14 ❖ Problems encountered with shared services

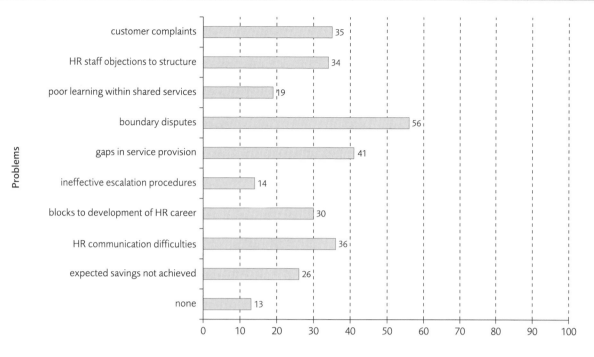

Source: CIPD survey (2007)

develop their skills. Finally, as the survey indicated and as was highlighted in one organisation, commercial expertise was being learned in administrative and operational roles. These skills could be deployed in non-HR jobs in business teams, if cuts in shared services numbers persisted.

On the challenges faced when introducing shared services, the issues highlighted in the survey (boundary disputes, gaps in services and communication problems) were covered earlier. As Figure 14 shows, in addition, a third of organisations reported customer complaints over the service. Pleasing the customer is not always easy. One case-study participant reported that managers think that they are the only customer and forget the rest of the organisation's needs. Keeping customers on side is especially critical for shared services, because if things do not go well in shared services, it affects the overall HR performance. As one respondent remarked, all HR services 'get lumped together' as poor if the administrative part malfunctions. This is a well-recognised requirement: HR has to get the basics right if it is to claim a seat at the top table.

A third of respondents also identified problems with HR staff objections to the new service. This fits with the 38% of organisations that reported no change in HR staff satisfaction, reported in Table 2. As we will describe in Chapter 10, there were examples given by case-study participants of where HR colleagues resisted restructuring, and it would appear that the creation of shared services was a focus of the objections.

From the case-study research, one additional problem was identified. An interviewee complained that their shared service centre was good at doing those things that were in the public eye but were less effective at the behind-the-scenes basics. Unevenness of performance has been reported elsewhere. For example, undertaking tasks governed by SLAs gets the attention that it deserves, but at the expense of other important matters. How serious this 'displacement' effect is depends upon how well the SLA has been constructed, so that it is comprehensive and/or well targeted on key processes.

> An international company found that its performance and reward system was driving the wrong behaviours in its HR shared services centre. Reward was based on customer metrics: the happier the customer, the bigger the payout to the service centre staff. This had the effect of causing the staff to go overboard helping customers even in violation of their own procedures. For example, payroll adjustments were made manually after payroll deadlines. This meant that subsequent adjustments had to be made, involving extra work and with the risk of errors (Reilly and Williams, 2006).

IMPLICATIONS

Any implementation of change is problematic and there is nothing unusual in the struggles reported here in organisations introducing new roles in new structures. Generally, organisations seemed positive with what they had created, and some of the difficulties identified in earlier research did not feature in case-study discussions or elicit much of a response in the survey. Where there have been challenges, they have varied according to the different roles.

Although only a quarter of survey respondents identified a lack of clarity in the business partner role as a problem they faced, it still seems that there are definitional problems. These manifest themselves in the interfaces between corporate HR and business heads. It may be that it is a fact of life that the business partner will struggle in this regard, but the difficulties in recruiting to the role, developing the right skills and coping with those that labour with the strategic input, suggest that not all is well. From the survey, this seems to be less of a customer challenge than an internal HR one, and is probably related to some of the structural problems we reported earlier. Thus, there were concerns laterally across the business partner population: as to how they can communicate effectively to stop them becoming too narrowly focused, and how they can manage upwards between the corporate centre and the business unit. The challenge faced in dealing with this tension was 'like walking a tightrope over the San Andreas fault', according to the former HR director of Hampshire County Council – and from the perspective of the business partners themselves, of being at risk of being 'hung, drawn and quartered by both sides'.

These difficulties manifest themselves even more with those in the centres of expertise, in light of the reported problems of communication and task segmentation. Further, the resourcing challenge comes through strongly, nearly a third of organisations identifying hiring difficulties. With the right staff, it seems the experts can bring real value to the organisation through their professional expertise and in their support to business partners. As we remarked earlier, centres of expertise are not suitable for everyone – perhaps not for small organisations or those perhaps with simple HR policies or processes (or where they are set elsewhere). The fact that learning and development is the most popular centre of expertise does show, however, that specialist contributions can be valuable to a wider range of organisations than one might think.

> '...that learning and development is the most popular centre of expertise does show... that specialist contributions can be valuable to a wider range of organisations than one might think.'

Few organisations seem to rate the importance of administration, yet a lot of time is spent on these activities and in determining the best delivery mechanism. Moreover, it is understood that administrative failure negatively rebounds on the function as a whole. The significant minority reporting customer complaints is an issue that should be addressed. The message from this research is that organisations need to get the whole delivery model to work if the shared services element is to prosper as well, given the challenges too in managing boundaries, communication and gaps in service provision. Yet the findings on HR staff objections also give pause for thought. Staff need to feel well-disposed towards their work, especially in customer-facing roles. Running down the administrative role is not the best way to obtain the best employee response, especially if there is a threat of outsourcing hanging over them.

Finally, looking at the survey results in a positive manner, three quarters of organisations did not select the questionnaire option that cost savings had not materialised, and the case studies could also point to reduction in HR costs. Nevertheless, for the quarter of organisations that had not achieved this goal with shared services, there should be particular concern. It can be argued that one of the principal purposes of shared services is to reduce expenditure, so this goal has to be achieved not at the expense of quality but together with it.

LEARNING POINTS

✤ If HR transformation is to work, the whole model has to operate successfully and in particular the relationships between the discrete parts. This means that good horizontal communication within HR units (eg among the business partners and centres of expertise) and between them (eg between shared service centres and centres of expertise), as well as vertical communication through the organisation from top to bottom is essential.

✤ Having centres of expertise is a useful means of integrating discrete people management activities, including traditional HR, OD, and learning and development.

✤ Hiring good-quality business partners is probably the best solution to the difficulties of performing the role well, but acknowledgement should be made of the tensions that these role-holders have to manage between business unit and corporate management.

✤ Administrative expertise is important to the success of the function and should not be downgraded on the basis that it does not add 'strategic' value.

RELATIONSHIPS WITH STAKEHOLDERS

7

❖ **In relation to CEOs HR's principal contribution is the 'ability to offer an independent perspective' (according to HR managers). Its weakest area is the quality of HR processes.**

❖ **The division of people management responsibilities between HR and the line is largely unchanged since 2003, despite HR's wish to have more work transferred to line managers.**

❖ **The principal reasons for HR's lack of success in transferring work to the line appear to be line manager priorities, their skills, the time available to them for people management tasks and poor manager self-service.**

INTRODUCTION

Our earlier report looked at HR's relationship with line managers, noting that the boundary between what line management does and what HR does is never a settled one. Nevertheless, the primary goal of HR for over 20 years has been the shift of activities from HR to managers. However, the people management contribution of line managers has varied greatly by work area. Furthermore, research (Torrington, 1998; CIPD, 2003) suggests that at the macro level, not much has changed in the relationship between HR and the line.

Although it is to be expected that e-HR and HR restructuring will result in future change, the impact may be mixed. Intranets and self-service have led to improved communication; they allow the function to move away from involvement in day-to-day administrative work. However, this may result in managers being more likely to resent having ill-designed processes 'dumped' upon them. Regarding structural change, on the one hand, the segmentation of activities signposts to managers when they should contact HR and for what; on the other hand, it introduces multiple channels rather than a one-stop shop.

Overall, the combined effect of structural and process change is often to reduce the number or the quality of line interactions with HR staff, particularly at a face-to-face level.

It is a moot point whether HR's push for devolution to the line is accepted by managers themselves. Managers have expressed doubts about their skills in dealing with people, managing employee behaviour or managing difficult issues with employees. Some were anxious about feeling exposed through inexperience or lack of knowledge or capability. Often, it is said that managers lack time to focus on people management responsibilities, exacerbated by change such as downsizing, delayering and globalisation. Moreover, there is evidence that line managers do not accept that people management is an important part of their job, frequently preferring not to engage in the 'messy stuff' of people management.

It may be that there are clear limits to the devolution of HR, driven by competence and efficiency, especially if there are few incentives for line managers to engage in people management activities as opposed to meeting business objectives.

> '...resistance to devolution of HR work does not only apply to managers – it comes from HR too.'

However, it should be noted that the resistance to devolution of HR work does not only apply to managers – it comes from HR too. There is research to suggest that some members of the HR function have been reluctant to devolve, due to concerns about losing power and control, giving up activities that they were good at, fears about job security if line managers prove to be too proficient, and concerns that managers were ill-equipped to deal with people management issues (Cunningham and Hyman, 1999).

RESEARCH RESULTS

Relationships with senior executives

In the 2007 survey, as in 2003, we asked where the CEO would 'score', on a five-point scale, the performance of HR on a number of dimensions. Because this is HR's view of what the CEO might think, the results must be treated with a certain

THE CHANGING HR FUNCTION

Figure 15 ❖ **'How do you think your CEO would score the performance of the HR function?'**

Mean score

−2 strongly negative   −1 negative   0 neither negative nor positive   1 positive   2 strongly positive

Source: CIPD survey (2007)

amount of caution! Figure 15 indicates that HR thinks the CEO would give good marks to the function in all areas. What perhaps is more interesting is where HR thinks the reaction would be not quite as positive. The quality of HR processes has the lowest proportion ticking the strongly positive box (12%) and the highest negative results (also 12%). Around a third was also not positive about HR's influence on board decisions, and there were several write-in comments about a lack of support from the board on HR issues. This seems to be connected to a wider point made by some survey participants that there is a lack of appreciation of the contribution that HR function can and should make and an absence of a shared vision towards people management. Nevertheless, in three areas the results had improved from 2003 – contribution to business performance, influence on board decisions, and closeness to the business.

Indeed, HR's strongest contribution seems to be the 'ability to offer an independent perspective'. A number of respondents also wrote something similar to this when commenting on HR's purpose. The advisory role encompasses a risk management element – HR's purpose is 'to advise and guide business in the area of HR and minimise risk to the business', to quote another respondent. This returns us to the discussion on HR's role. Clearly, the relationship HR has is dependent upon its positioning in the organisation and its accepted contribution.

Relationships with line managers

In many organisations HR has been trying to rebalance its relationships with line managers. The aim has been to make the line managers both more self-reliant, not as dependent on

HR, and more attentive to their people management responsibilities. Our survey tried to establish whether or not there has been a shift since the CIPD's 2003 research in the division of responsibility between HR and the line over a range of questions.

Table 3, opposite, shows there has been less of a change than one might expect.

What is apparent is that HR still takes the lead on some subjects, the line on others, whereas for a third group matters are more shared. Thus with respect to remuneration and implementing redundancies, HR takes the lead in roughly two thirds of organisations, whereas work organisation is much more an issue for line management to claim responsibility. The other areas are shared, though with the lead assumed more by the line on recruitment and by HR on employee relations and training and development.

These results suggest that HR has not pushed responsibility to the line as much as the rhetoric of change would suggest. In other words, HR has been comfortable in still undertaking a range of operational people management tasks. An alternative explanation is that line managers have failed to pick up the baton that has been passed to them. We tried to tease out the answer to this question in the survey by asking whether it was HR's intention to go further in devolution terms. The reply was instructive: nearly three quarters would have gone further in passing responsibility to managers.

This, then, begs the question of what has inhibited this devolution process (see Figure 16, opposite). We tried to probe whether the source of the difficulty was line managers

Work area	2003			2007		
	Line/ mainly line	Shared	Mainly HR/ HR	Line/ mainly line	Shared	Mainly HR/ HR
Recruitment/selection	31	52	17	29	55	16
Pay and benefits	8	29	62	7	28	65
Employee relations	8	40	52	6	40	54
Training and development	12	44	43	10	49	42
Implementing redundancies	6	34	59	4	34	62
Work organisation*				54	37	9

Table 3 ❖ The allocation of responsibility to line management in how decisions are taken

*This question was not asked in 2003
Source: CIPD (2003, 2007)

themselves, HR, or failed technology. Maybe not surprisingly, these senior HR respondents did not see HR as the primary cause of the problem, although over 40% identified the function's 'reluctance to let go' as part of the issue. The principal culprits were line manager priorities (top of the list),

skills and time available and poor self-service (employee or manager). Line training and disposition contributed to quite an extent, as did their bosses' own lack of encouragement to tackle people management issues. A lack of role clarity and HR's own policies and practices were blamed to a lesser extent.

Figure 16 ❖ 'What has restricted progress in the HR function?'

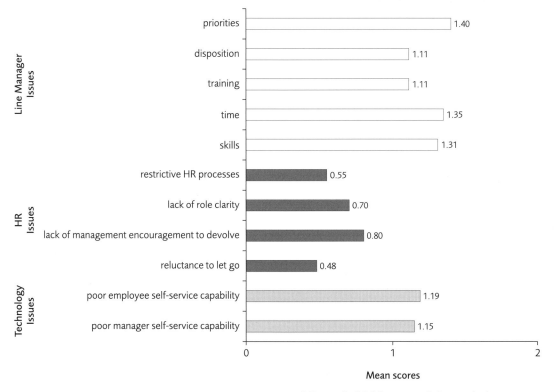

Source: CIPD survey (2007)

In some ways there was a similar pattern of responses from the case-study participants. As one HR director admitted, 'We still don't have the right relationship with the line.' There were worries over the conception of the line's people management role and interface with HR, and over HR's response to these difficulties.

At Ernst & Young, for example, concern was expressed that line managers do not fully 'own' the people strategy. In part, the problem, according to another organisation, was because it was hard to keep senior management 'sticking to the party line' and to get them to give support when resistance occurred or things went wrong. This echoes the results of other CIPD research on the line's role in relation to reward (Purcell and Hutchinson, 2007). The authors comment that a 'surprising number' of line managers do not accept the need for controls over remuneration (eg merit pay, bonuses and promotions) in part because 'they can blame "the system" for any constraints on their actions'.

The head of HR at Firefly worried that although most managers took their people management responsibilities seriously, some needed 'reminding'. She had to keep emphasising that HR was there as a 'sounding board', not a replacement of the line. But she also acknowledged that in the eyes of managers there is a 'fuzzy line' between their role and that of HR. Another HR manager said that too often managers asked 'What is HR doing about this problem?' rather than 'What can I do to solve it?'

In a surprising degree of vehemence, more junior members of the HR community described their relationships with the line in much more negative terms. Quotes from different organisations included:

> *The line always wants someone to watch their back or to dig them out of holes.*

> *We in HR should have a toddler's taming guide to deal with line managers.*

> *Some managers want to do as little as possible in managing their staff.*

We were not able to uncover whether these views were shared or rejected by more senior HR management, or indeed whether they were aware of the stridency of these opinions.

> **'The problem was compounded by a tendency for HR to find it hard to let go, as well as to avoid upsetting customers.'**

Regarding the boundaries between the activities carried out by the line and HR, there was some anxiety at Ernst & Young that managers could be reluctant to take on employee-related administrative tasks, even where manager self-service worked well. Similarly, at Fujitsu

Services managers might try to involve business partners in operational or administrative tasks they should do themselves. The problem was compounded by a tendency for HR to find it hard to let go, as well as to avoid upsetting customers. Moreover, there was a sense in which HR accepted that it had to 'oil the wheels of business', not throw a spanner in the works.

There is a balance to be struck between encouraging line manager independence through growing their confidence and self-reliance (an objective of the HR director of Surrey County Council) and ensuring that corporate policy and principles are acted upon. This tension was addressed by Nortel, for example, by giving managers more freedom to act but within a narrower set of rules.

In the light of this background it is entirely consistent for HR's response to be to invest in line manager training and support mechanisms precisely to build their self-confidence. Capita, for example, intends to run one-day workshops to help managers understand what their role is in managing their own people and how it can best be undertaken. E.ON has online tools which support those managers who are comfortable using the self-serve processes. These tools include, among other things, clear policy and guidance documents to support them in their roles.

> Vodafone has sought to re-emphasise the people management responsibilities of managers. The managers are described as being 'primarily accountable for the whole employee life cycle' and for those processes that impact directly on the people strategy and 'employee experience'. To assist them, in the UK HR has developed a toolkit for line managers on their people management responsibilities. This toolkit was developed following focus groups with employees on what they wanted from their managers. Also in the UK, managers get 360-degree inputs on their people management performance, and employee engagement results are also used by HR business partners to point out where managers are doing well or not so well in connecting with their staff.

The philosophy underlying this skill development was succinctly put by the Hampshire County Council HR director – 'The more HR develops the line, the less the line needs HR.' Although some would see this as an existential threat to the function, as our earlier discussion on HR's purpose suggests, most HR directors hope that HR can then concentrate on bigger, wider, more long-term questions relating to how people management performance can be lifted.

Relationships with employees

It should be clear from the research results already reported that HR does not want to usurp the role of the line manager in relationships with staff or be seen in opposition to the rest of management. This is borne out in the answers in the survey to the question of whether the function accepts Ulrich's 'employee champion' notion. In the CIPD's 2003 survey, less than 10% of respondents wanted in future to play the employee champion role (CIPD, 2003). In the 2007 survey, only 8% of respondents thought that helping employees was HR's most important task, and in nearly 800 written responses to the question of HR's purpose, nobody mentioned championing employees and only two saw HR's role as 'to encourage and facilitate employee voice'. Comparison between this survey and that in 2003 shows that in responses to two questions (what should drive change in people management policies and practices, and where HR wants to be in future), the function wants to be even more business- and less employee-driven.

Nevertheless, in the chapter on HR's purpose it was apparent that – through employee engagement and wellness, in particular – in some organisations HR wanted to improve the employer/employee relationship at collective level. What is inhibiting HR from playing this role is, according to some (such as an attendee of the CIPD discussion group in Dublin), HR's remoteness from the workforce. This has a number of causes, including:

❖ the introduction of call and service centres, located at a distance from employees, and the removal of local administrative staff

❖ the strategic role of business partners leaving no time and less inclination to deal with individual employee needs (apart from those at executive level)

❖ the automation of processes that previously would have required interaction between HR and employees

❖ the devolution of people management responsibilities to line managers and the emphasis on their taking charge of employee issues

❖ an emphasis HR has put on its alignment with business priorities.

Purcell and Hutchinson (2007), in their research for the CIPD on the line management role in learning and development, put this argument clearly, noting that the danger of too much decentralisation to the line, and the development of online systems through a shared service model, is that it 'removes the "human" from "human resource" management'.

Some of the organisations participating in the research showed signs either of picking up the negative consequences of HR transformation for staff or of a vital need to emphasise the quality of employee relationships. The type of response varied. For example, Cable and Wireless explicitly moved back from a 'low-touch, high-tech' environment to a 'higher-touch' environment, its HR professionals becoming more closely

involved with line managers. The E.ON work on the limits of the effectiveness of automation described earlier demonstrates another case of acknowledging the benefits of human interaction. Ernst & Young seems to recognise that being a 'people' organisation fits the nature of its work activity and employee base, and that as a consequence HR should be well resourced. Similarly, at Firefly good personal interactions are an important part of the organisation's culture. Vodafone testifies to the employee relations benefits of an effective call centre, and the existence of case management units at Surrey County Council and HMRC provide the means by which HR can assist employees as well line managers.

> '...the distinction between the collective and the individual does not work where everybody knows each other.'

Moreover, one interviewee at least – the HR manager at Firefly – was happy to embrace the employee champion role without equivocation. This seemed to be in large part because her relationships with most employees were personal. She knew everyone and they knew her. She wanted to be seen as approachable and able to sort out their problems, although the emphasis of her work remains trying to coach their managers to be able to sort out any of their issues, thereby, as elsewhere, taking on more people management responsibility. The fact that this is a small company might illustrate that the distinction between the collective and the individual does not work where everybody knows each other.

IMPLICATIONS

Dealing with employees

The conclusion one can draw from these results with respect to HR's relationships with employees is that in large organisations the function does not deal with them as individuals but in a collective form only. HR is increasingly interested in employee engagement, commitment and motivation, at a collective level, and how these link to organisational performance. But the danger is that HR becomes too theoretical with no understanding of the practical reality of its own policies and practices within the organisation. The logic of HR's position that line managers should deal with staff at the individual level cannot be faulted, but this comes at a cost, and possibly one that has not yet been fully realised.

There is a bind here for HR: it is the function that should know about employees – why they come to work, why they stay, what motivates them. How does it develop this intelligence if it does not come into contact with staff, but rather is reliant on whether managers articulate employee needs (potentially less than objective) or on the results of attitude surveys (which can be a rather blunt instrument)? This loss of the 'human face' of

HR does trouble some practitioners. For these HR managers, although there are benefits from consolidation, automation and devolution, there are unfortunate consequences.

So how can HR be aware of employee needs without championing them or interfering in the legitimate role of the line manager? Some face-to-face interaction via focus groups and 'town meetings' could, perhaps, supplement running regular employee attitude surveys and listening to line managers, tracking calls to help lines/counselling services and systematically analysing the results. Attempts could also be made to mitigate the effects of depersonalisation. Those working in the HR shared service centre at Ernst & Young tried to build trust and get across to managers and employees that it was 'a person at the end of the phone, not a voice'. The same can be true for employees.

Moreover, is it not right for HR to step in if there is a breakdown in the relationship between the manager and employee, when managers do not give sufficient attention to people issues or manage staff insensitively? In some organisations, this role described in Chapter 6 is explicitly acknowledged. Whether it is acknowledged or not, should not HR feel empowered to tackle managers with the wrong attitudes to colleagues and insist that they perform their people management role?

Task allocation to line managers

The other critical, and linked, question concerns devolution – the passing of responsibility from HR to the line. Some people do not like the term 'devolution' because managers are the real owners of employee relationships, not HR. However, the alternative suggestions – 'transfer', 'assignment' – give the same impression that people management responsibilities are in HR's gift to transfer/assign/devolve.

Whatever the term, devolution is all about who does what. Do managers interview and select new recruits? Do they deal with poor performance? Do they conduct return-to-work interviews after an employee's sickness absence? Do they hold meetings with employee representatives on work organisation or HR policy? The answer from this research is that not much seems to have changed since the 2003 survey (or indeed from the Torrington research of 1998) in the balance of what HR does, what the line does and what is done in partnership. Not surprisingly, the division of labour, as ever, depends upon the topic.

However, the desire of HR to devolve more activities to the line still burns brightly. This may be because it can allow HR numbers to be cut. It may concern the balance of HR's work. In the survey, 71% of the senior HR respondents cited line management support as one of the three most time-consuming tasks, compared with 37% who gave this activity as one of the three most important. There may be a more philosophical objective to ensure that managers discharge their essential people management

responsibilities (Legge, 1989). HR may be convinced of the business benefits if managers give more attention to their staff. The balance in the argument varies by organisation.

> '...the desire of HR to devolve more activities to the line still burns brightly.'

The obstacles to getting devolution to work better also seem to be unchanged – manager priorities, skills and time, more than HR's reluctance to let go. As other CIPD findings (on technology and on line manager roles) have suggested, this research confirms the risk that managers will feel 'dumped upon' if HR tries to shift administrative, as much as operational, responsibilities onto managers. This resentment is compounded if the technological inadequacies of self-service make the task harder.

But is it a bad thing that devolution has not progressed faster? At one level we do not think so. HR keeps pushing for devolution without standing back and reviewing what should be the balance between HR and the line, not in an ideal world but given the people management limitations of many managers and what is best in terms of organisational efficiency. If management and HR are working in partnership on a range of issues, that is healthy and not a cause for concern because it might deliver the best result for the organisation. The precise allocation of responsibilities should depend on line manager capability, the business model and the sort of staff employed. Those organisations that rely heavily on the capability of their staff for business success may be prepared to invest more in HR, to ensure that there is proper attention given to employees. Other organisations would say that they cannot afford such an overhead and have to rely on their managers being effective.

Indeed, this is what we saw in this research: two very different approaches to line management expressed through the role of the business partners. One school of thought has hands-on, very much engaged, business partners who seem to be very critical to the employee value proposition. By contrast, another school of thought saw line managers as much more responsible for people management, operating in more of a self-help environment. The business partner was the back stop – if all else fails, then management would turn to them.

Reframing the relationship

HR can move to a better relationship with line management through a number of inter-related actions. HR needs to build mutual trust with managers, develop their people management skills, secure the support of senior management and, if it is to deploy manager self-service as a tool in changing task responsibility, it has to ensure that the technology is effective.

Building trust

Irrespective of the approach, as a Capita line manager put it: 'Success comes from mutual respect' between the line and HR. So we would worry about the negative comments relating to line managers, reported earlier, made by some HR staff. Their frustration is evident; the cause is less so, but there is an apparent gap between the rhetoric of HR transformation and how it is perceived on the ground. If we went into the same organisations and asked a cross-section of line managers, they might well complain of cumbersome and obstructive HR policies and slow and inefficient HR processes, as has been reported in other research (eg Whittaker and Marchington, 2003). These differences of perspective may be a fact of organisational life, but it also shows that there is still hard work to be done in getting more realistic expectations of what HR expects of line management and what line management can be expected to deliver. Mutual respect and trust will not occur if this does not happen.

Building capability

But what should HR do if there are genuine deficiencies in the line's people management capabilities? HR should continue to offer training and guidance to managers and organise workshops to tackle difficult issues. There are good examples of how to do this in the research reported earlier. This effort should be focused on those areas where line management engagement is most sought – eg performance management and reward. The 2006 CIPD reward survey (CIPD, 2006c) found that line manager skills was the main inhibitor to reward implementation and this was confirmed in more recent CIPD research (Purcell and Hutchinson, 2007), but how much of a challenge this is depends on what managers are being asked to do. Nonetheless, managers themselves need to skill up and recognise their responsibilities.

> '...managers themselves need to skill up and recognise their responsibilities.'

Getting people management capability as a key part of selection for posts and induction and refresher training can be supported by its assessment in performance appraisal and its use in bonus decisions (with 360-degree inputs?). This would both send a strong signal that people management is important in the organisation and offer incentives to managers to take it seriously (an important missing factor in getting attention given to people management, according to McGovern et al, 1997).

Securing high-level commitment

We would also argue that greater effort should be devoted to getting top management on board and to avoiding situations where senior managers do not allow their line colleagues to deal with people as they would wish because of the way that their business objectives are specified (Cunningham and Hyman, 1999).

Firstly, HR must ensure that the executive level understands the importance of people to organisational performance. Some of our case studies were working very hard to get this message through, demanding that attention be given to employee engagement and the employer brand, but as the survey responses made plain, the backing of the CEO 'is not always there'.

Secondly, CEOs will have to recognise the contribution of the HR function and give it their support. The possibility that CEOs embrace HR's independent advice is welcome. If true, it would confirm findings from the CIPD's research on re-organising (Whittington and Molloy, 2005) that HR has a role second only to Finance in managing reorganisations.

Thirdly, senior management has to send the signal that line managers are indeed people managers with the responsibility and accountability for the people issues in their area.

If this happens, HR will get more support for giving attention to interpersonal skills at manager selection. And, as Hutchinson and Purcell report (2007) in relation to learning and development, if senior managers 'get it' in terms of the critical nature of people development, they can give vital support to hard-pressed line colleagues. They point out that

> It's nearly impossible to exaggerate the importance of senior management support and action on the development of line managers, and through them, on the climate of learning and development in the organisation.

Getting the technological balance correct

The technology has to be right if managers are to be more effective, not weighed down by administrative trivia. Sometimes managers' negative feelings are because HR has not communicated its purpose well. For example, it should be possible to demonstrate the benefits of automating a task that was previously done manually by managers. Where the task was previously done by HR and managers are now being asked to do it, the challenge is whether it is right to expect time-pressed (and expensive) managers to carry out tasks performed by less expensive staff whose job is to administer clerical tasks. So manager self-service has to work as billed technically, but also in terms of what it is reasonable to ask managers to do.

LEARNING POINTS

❖ HR should work towards getting senior management to accept the value of people to the success of the organisation, the role of the line in managing their staff and the contribution HR can make to facilitating the employer/employee relationship.

❖ HR should critically assess line management capability in people management and, depending upon the answer, be prepared to:

  ❖ invest in skills training

  ❖ offer practical day-to-day support

  ❖ coach and encourage their contribution

  ❖ transfer them back to specialist roles.

❖ A single approach to managers may not be appropriate, so be prepared to offer more HR resource to some business units than others on the basis of the above capability assessment and the business imperatives.

❖ Build trust and mutual respect between HR and the line even if this means accepting some managerial deficiencies, but do not tolerate the misuse of staff.

❖ Consider different means of discovering employee attitudes to their work and employer without cutting across the role of their line managers.

MEASURING HR PERFORMANCE   8

- ❖ **Virtually all organisations measured HR's efficiency, and over half examined HR effectiveness through people management practice and its effect on outcomes such as absence.**

- ❖ **HR and people management performance were measured through business performance, surveys of managers/employees and customer satisfaction metrics.**

- ❖ **Results were reported in a number of ways and frequencies.**

- ❖ **System or policy evaluation did not appear to be particularly common.**

INTRODUCTION

Our earlier report (CIPD, 2006a) observed that HR has been under increasing pressure to demonstrate value and, as a consequence, there has been a greater emphasis on quality data collection. Measuring HR performance may have an effect on the relationship between HR and the rest of the organisation. The new approach to measuring HR work demanded by a more explicit demonstration of value has resulted in some organisations shifting from soft contracting between HR and its customers to hard contracting. One advantage of hard contracting is that it can bring commercial thinking to providing HR services, although the disadvantage is that potentially bureaucracy increases and flexibility is compromised.

Despite all the research interest in the measurement of human capital and the contribution of people management to organisational success, there appears to be limited practical application. It appears that few organisations assess the strategic contribution of people management and link it to organisational performance. For example, recent research (IRS, 2006) found that in the majority of organisations, most measurement is confined to assessing operational efficiency. This may be connected to the above point that customer satisfaction is evaluated in terms of meeting SLA targets and it is that which defines the performance of the function. This was backed up by a 2006 survey in *Personnel Today*, which showed that around 40% of respondents did not see measuring human capital as an organisational priority. There is also more anecdotal evidence that HR has been focused on the cost of the function and in metrics such as the ratio of HR staff numbers to total employee numbers. The conclusion to be drawn is that HR needs to develop better metrics looking at its own effectiveness and impact, and to build analytical models on the link between people management and business performance if it is to become a true strategic partner.

RESEARCH RESULTS

Efficiency versus effectiveness

In the survey, we tested out the question whether HR was measured on both its effectiveness and its efficiency, and how it established these results. Virtually all the survey respondents measured HR's efficiency in one way or another, although there were a small number that wrote in to the effect that 'little robust or formal performance effectiveness was undertaken.' Half the sample looked at functional costs and at the HR/employee ratio. A slightly larger proportion looked at HR effectiveness through people management practice and its effect on outcomes such as absence.

> **'Virtually all the survey respondents measured HR's efficiency in one way or another...'**

As to the metrics used to establish these results, efficiency was measured in a number of ways – through business performance (half the survey), surveys of managers or employees to customer satisfaction metrics (a third of the survey). The pattern of assessing effectiveness was very similar, although line manager inputs were stronger. Employee surveys seem to be particularly important in looking at people management practice, which is appropriate, given that these should pick up the impact of line management as well as HR. Sixty per cent of respondents use business performance measures to look at the impact of HR on organisational performance. As for the quality of HR services, half the survey took note of line manager views and two fifths of employee opinion.

Case-study organisations are using similar techniques. Capita – as befits a service provider of outsourced HR activities – reports service levels on a weekly basis for its administrative centre and it provides regular monthly performance statistics for managers (eg on headcount per business unit, starters and leavers, grievances, disciplinary cases, turnover, sickness and long-term absence). Firefly uses the dashboard method to highlight people management performance. This includes number of sick days in the past month, length of service, retention statistics, plus a statement of all current activity, such as recruitment, pay rises, promotions. Also reported are a breakdown of how HR time is spent and current or forthcoming HR projects.

There is also measurement of employee engagement by case-study organisations and a link made to organisational performance, as exemplified by the boxed example below.

> Vodafone has created in the UK an employee engagement index to measure the employee experience. This allows tracking of employee engagement over time, compared internally by function and externally against norms. It also permits a measure of assessment of employee experience initiatives. The index is linked to business results and forms part of an HR balanced scorecard (the other headings being *financial performance*, *internal processes* and *customer experience*).

Customer experience and service levels

As for customer feedback, Capita has a feedback question in its manager self-service system. Similarly, Hampshire County Council issues a questionnaire after each internal consultancy assignment and has a formal review each year at departmental level of HR's performance. Customer forums with senior management participation are also used to get their views on services, and also give them understanding of what HR is trying to do. This has helped get a better alignment between business need and HR policy development, and to move towards more 'sensible' discussion on HR performance. Surrey County Council phones customers after they have used the duty (help) desk. Fujitsu Services uses a pulse survey for constant feedback and HR effectiveness surveys to gain further detailed feedback on topical areas identified through HR effectiveness reviews.

> HMRC has a Service Improvement team that encompasses the following three key areas.

> ❖ HR IT improvement and development that is designed to offer a better technological service to customers
>
> ❖ an HR customer service manager, who feeds back issues from business partners and directors relating to the HR service
>
> ❖ an HR performance development manager who leads on improving the skills of the HR service centre staff.
>
> The overall aim is to link into one of the key objectives of 'the HMRC Ambition', to improve service to the internal customer.

SLAs are used to define service standards with customers and then to measure performance against the standards. Reviewing performance with customers can be a useful way of getting some feedback. Vodafone says that the SLA process helps ensure a good service quality. Another organisation found that defining its achievable standards only demonstrated that the customer demands might exceed what was possible with constrained resources. The example given was the SLA requirement to issue an offer letter within three days, but in some parts of the business the market is so competitive that an offer letter has to be issued the same day.

Evaluation

There is research (eg Cabrera and Cabrera, 2003) that suggests that HR is not particularly good at evaluation of change initiatives – new policies, practices or structures. A number of the survey respondents made comments to this effect. However, we also saw some good examples of structural and process review. The MOD had a formal review of its HR structure, with particular emphasis on the role of the business partner. As described earlier, E.ON looked at how well the automation of some processes was working. Best value or similar assessments used in the public sector can be useful to evaluate strengths and weaknesses in performance. Firefly uses its dashboard, referred to earlier, to evaluate changes over time in people management performance. The company (like others in the research) has an annual employee engagement survey that measures the effectiveness of many HR practices. In the survey, some organisations reported using benchmarking techniques, but it was not clear whether this was to evaluate the quality of HR or merely to compare on efficiency measures, such as ratios.

This illustrates one of the difficulties organisations face in moving from measuring performance to evaluating the success of people management practice to drive change or affirm that the status quo is working.

IMPLICATIONS

These results are welcome in that virtually all the organisations in the survey are measuring the performance of HR at least in some way. They suggest that many HR organisations are assessing people management in broad terms, not narrow functional terms, and that effectiveness and impact are as important as efficiency and process quality. Whereas costs and ratios are used to measure HR efficiency, equal proportions are looking at outcomes, including on organisational performance. What is not clear is how many organisations are building a model of the link between people performance and organisational performance. As indicated above, some of our case studies are interested in employee engagement and using its results to influence policy and practice, but the fact that only a quarter of the survey use them to examine the impact of HR on organisational performance suggests that employee engagement models are not that common.

> 'What is not clear is how many organisations are building a model of the link between people performance and organisational performance.'

We would suggest that the way forward for HR is to combine the efficiency measures that look at how well processes are done and how costly the function is, with ways of looking at how effective the HR function is and separately how effective the people management effort is. Some commentators (eg Boudreau and Ramstad, 2003) would also look at the impact of people management to reinforce the fact that it can deliver organisational benefits.

This research suggests that HR is moving in the right direction, but that more is to be done. Firstly, it should be acknowledged that is very difficult to measure the effectiveness (let alone impact) of the *HR function* and its contribution to business performance, because it is particularly difficult to establish cause and effect. Secondly, one problem is that 'softer' qualitative measures, such as a survey of line managers' assessments of HR's performance, do not necessarily capture the level of performance being sought. There may be a difference between the manager view of success and the corporate view. For example, a manager may mark HR down for not giving him/her the advice on, say, a disciplinary case he/she wanted, but the effectiveness of the function should on this occasion have been marked up because HR is challenging the line and giving guidance that is beneficial to the whole organisation.

When Becker and Huselid (1999) tried to look at the impact of the HR function, they ended up, not surprisingly, with a qualitative approach. Successful HR seemed to be a combination of what HR managers can do as individuals in their awareness, what their function can achieve in terms of service, and how HR can drive cultural change within the wider organisation.

The argument with respect to *people management* and its impact on organisational performance is quite different. There is a plethora of research that indicates that a number of people management practices are associated with superior organisational performance (eg Purcell *et al*, 2003). One view (eg Huselid, 1995) is that there are 'bundles' of practice that if implemented will deliver organisational benefits. The sort of practices that have an effect get grouped under a number of headings – eg high skill requirements, discretion at work, teamworking and incentives (Tamkin, 2005). However, in our view these 'bundles' must fit the organisational context. Indeed, research suggests that competitive advantage comes from getting a good 'fit' between people management practices and organisational requirements, rather than the practice *per se*. This emphasises the need to examine what leads to success in a particular organisation, perhaps segmented by location, activity or occupational group. It has to be acknowledged, though, that establishing best fit is harder than describing best practice.

> '...research suggests that competitive advantage comes from getting a good "fit" between people management practices and organisational requirements...'

There has been criticism that there is a lack of agreement on what constitutes the bundles of practices. This may however simply be a reflection of the fact that the mix will differ with the organisation. Yet specific practices have been identified in the aerospace industry and the service profit chain has been used in customer service organisations in retail, banking and telecommunications. In the service sector, the argument has been taken to a higher level by advancing the case that there is a causal link between employee engagement/commitment and business performance.

Thus, HR should be collecting data to feed its employment model, not just to pick out which policies and practices are working well. This is not to say that the function should not test customer reaction (employee and manager) to the services it offers. It was somewhat surprising that more organisations are not using customer surveys, let alone other measures of customer satisfaction. Here, HR could learn from other functions where these tools are ever more sophisticated.

Finally, there is the question of evaluation of HR activity. There is no evidence to suggest that this is sufficiently frequently carried out either at the individual policy level or at the system level. If HR transformation is really to alter ways of doing things, there should be more attention to setting out the change goals and seeing whether these have been met, and adjusting if necessary. As the Deloitte (2005) report on HR transformation makes clear, success has been partial because of a failure to implement the model in full, take account of customers needs and deliver all aspects of fulfilling the business strategy. Organisations have to think through more clearly the consequences of the change, take that learning and apply it to further reconfiguration or development of the service.

Chapter 9 addresses this point in more detail.

LEARNING POINTS

- ❖ Distinguish between HR efficiency and effectiveness and find the most appropriate methods of assessment of each of them.

- ❖ Be clear about what the HR function is responsible for and what lies within line management's remit.

- ❖ Construct a set of metrics, based on human capital ones, that allows people management to be linked to organisational performance.

- ❖ Measure customer satisfaction with HR not just on transactional/operational services but in the added value area. In particular, find ways of assessing business partners' strategic contribution.

- ❖ Build in processes to evaluate the results of any major policy or change initiative, especially regarding the restructuring of HR itself. Establish at the outset the change objectives and the initial situation to make subsequent assessment of progress possible.

HR STAFF SKILLS AND DEVELOPMENT 9

❖ **There are different views between senior and junior members of the HR community over the career challenges in the function. The latter are more concerned than the former about the implications of new organisational structures.**

❖ **There has not been much change since 2003 in the skill needs of the function.**

❖ **Senior HR managers seem more concerned with the skills required of the business partners (such as political and influencing skills) than the general (interpersonal) skills required of the function.**

❖ **The emphasis on development appears to be more on formal training than experiential learning (ie through measures such as short-term assignments, project work and cover).**

INTRODUCTION

In our earlier report in this project, we explored a number of aspects of internal resourcing and development to meet the changing skill requirements. Firstly, we looked at the organisational choice between buying in HR expertise and bringing on home-grown staff. It would appear that many organisations were finding it difficult to fill key HR roles and looking to the external market: in particular, call centre, business partner and some specialist roles were seen as hard to fill.

The other choice we examined was between an 'HR professionals only' approach and one where organisations were happy to take in from the line or general management. There has always been transition into HR, but it would appear (Tamkin *et al*, 2006) that flows into the HR function have become more difficult as HR roles become more challenging and technical and the entry from administrative positions is more difficult. As to the separate matter of business partner positions being sourced from outside HR, opinion seems to be divided on the benefits of this approach.

A further development issue we examined was the extent to which there is a clear divide between specialists and generalists, each with their own career path, and whether (and how) links should be made between them. Under new HR structures, administrative specialists have been separated out into shared service centres (or outsourced), making it difficult for people to move out of administration and into other roles, whether as experts or business partners.

As for solutions, some organisations are looking at creating developmental posts or offering temporary assignments to help staff gain the necessary experience to be able to move to

a more senior or different role. Joining in cross-functional projects, covering for absent colleagues or shadowing a more senior person have been some of the approaches tried.

RESEARCH RESULTS

Career challenges

The most striking finding from this research appears to contradict earlier CIPD research (Tamkin *et al*, 2006). The overall impression from the survey was that structure had little impact on development upwards or sideways, or in joining the function. Two thirds of our survey respondents said that the changes gave more opportunity to staff, compared with only 17% who thought that it was harder to develop people into new roles.

> '...this research appears to contradict earlier CIPD research...Two thirds of our survey respondents said that the changes gave more opportunity to staff...'

This view was supported by the HR director at Capita. She felt that careers now had more structure to them than in the past.

When dealing with the same career issues in our HR staff focus groups, a different picture from the above emerges. Administrative staff in particular commented that career paths were not as easy as in the past. They pointed to the 'massive leap' between administrative roles to embedded HR roles or centres of expertise. The hope had been that staff could move from the shared service centre to an expert role, but this had not yet happened. Moreover, concern was expressed about business partners being 'owned' by their business unit, rather than by the function. This had the effect of preventing the development of a talent management programme for all HR staff and of leaving a lack of corporate knowledge of the HR talent pool. This was described as 'completely bonkers' by one respondent and 'a disgrace' by another.

Part of the differences between the two pieces of research may be explained by the fact that this survey was completed by senior HR managers and the focus group inputs come from more junior members of HR teams.

Response to challenges

Development difficulties for staff will emerge if there is no formal talent management approach for HR, if progress is too ad hoc rather than structured, or if the aspirations of staff to progress are thwarted. Specific examples where this had happened were given. In one organisation, support for CIPD training is provided for personnel officers and above, but not for administrative staff. In another organisation, the example was offered of a shared service centre colleague who was undertaking her CIPD training but finding it difficult to cover all the necessary work areas. In this organisation the embedded HR roles are always filled externally and never internally.

There was support for and understanding of these career challenges from some organisations. One organisation introduced its competency framework because of perceptions that the function did not do enough to develop staff and that there were impediments to career development.

Skill demands

As for the skills and competencies required, as was the case with devolution, we asked the same question in the 2007 survey as in 2003. Table 4, below, gives the comparative results.

There are differences in the results between the two surveys, but similarities too. Because these are not matched samples, interpretation should be cautious. The key changes are that business knowledge is recognised as more important in 2007 than in the 2003 survey, and, as to the most challenging, there have been noteworthy reversals in the ability to deliver against targets (less challenging) and willingness to innovate (more so).

Strategic thinking remains the most important competence, followed by influencing/political skills and business knowledge. This shows the emphasis on the business partner type of skill set in thinking at executive/senior HR level. Some of our case-study HR directors would add the importance of personal credibility and the need to make an impact as other

Table 4 ❖ **Assessment of the HR function's competencies/capabilities**

Competency	2003		2007	
	Most important (to HR's effectiveness) (%)	Biggest challenge (to developing these skills) (%)	Most important (to HR's effectiveness) (%)	Biggest challenge (to developing these skills) (%)
Influencing/political skills	61	64	51	58
Understanding of HR practices	26	10	27	8
Empathy/communication/listening skills	24	15	16	8
Leadership ability	35	26	34	34
Strategic thinking	46	48	54	53
Ability to deliver against targets	39	40	40	29
Business knowledge	32	34	49	38
Negotiating skills	11	19	8	11
Integrity	25	5	23	4
Willingness to innovate	13	17	17	34

Source: CIPD (2003, 2007)

THE CHANGING HR FUNCTION

key features, along with the 'customer-focused skills' to engage in the right debate with managers to influence the development of policies and strategies. Hampshire County Council's former HR director also identified a shortfall in helicopter skills: seeing the big picture and how everyone contributes to it.

The fact that willingness to innovate is seen as more challenging than before and ability to deliver against targets is less challenging further indicates where the emphasis in HR is moving towards – as seen from a senior HR perspective, at least. It is also worth noting that there is also a fair degree of congruence between importance and development need, except on those things that HR would be expected to be good at – understanding of HR practices, ability to deliver against targets, empathy/communication/listening skills and integrity – where development need does not match importance.

Development

Where there are skill gaps the question arises as to how to fill them. The survey asked just this question. Multiple answers were possible, and the results are shown in Figure 17, below. Nearly three quarters of respondents chose external courses, followed by CIPD study (57%) and half selected internal events and external conferences. The emphasis therefore seems to be

on more formal types of learning. Experiential development was not so strongly represented, project working used by just over a third of organisations and short-term assignments by a quarter of respondents. Using staff in temporary roles was only chosen by 13% of the survey. There were also a small number of participants who wrote in that coaching, networking, job swaps and development plans were used.

If this is indeed a fair reflection of the situation that experiential development is not as common as formal training, it is an important finding, given that education does not easily deal with gaps in soft skills. But perhaps, as the skills section suggested, HR directors do not see this as an area that needs attention.

Our case-study organisations reported rather more use of experiential development. Surrey County Council, for example, moves business partners around both for development reasons and to limit silo thinking. There is also rotation between the duty desk, case work and project roles that offers resourcing flexibility but also the broadening of skills. As for preparation for new roles, Reuters specifically identifies assignments for staff to test out whether they would make good business partners. Hampshire County Council helped those working in the centres of excellence to obtain exposure to the corporate centre. These staff were wary of working in the centre and changing role, so the HR director tried to give secondments into the centre and to gain

---

Figure 17 ❖ 'How are you closing skills gaps in HR?'

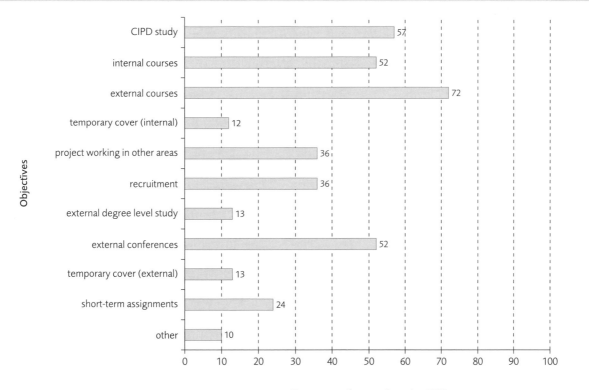

Percentage of respondents (n = 763)

Source: CIPD survey (2007)

experience through working on corporate projects. The Council is now looking at coaching and CPD opportunities. Capita's development was described as 'bespoke' – ie tailored to the individual. Mentors were appointed from within the HR team to identify knowledge, skills and experience gaps and guide development, including giving staff 'exposure' to the different businesses. Reuters also used mentors within HR to coach business partners, where appropriate. This contrasts with what was described as the 'self-help culture' at Ernst & Young that seems more characteristic of HR (Tamkin *et al*, 2006).

Formal training was also employed by the case-study organisations. Hampshire County Council put around 300 staff through a home-grown development programme. Further, all senior professional HR staff were required to complete CIPD study. Knowledge gaps may be filled during 'brown bag lunches'. Capita encourages external law updates and will also sponsor for professional qualifications. At Fujitsu Services all senior HR staff attend a three-day change course that outlines the company's philosophy of change management, as well as describing the change tools available. E.ON has an HR functional academy which supports the professional development of the function.

Use is also made of competency frameworks to assist with development (and if required performance management). Capita, for example, has a skills development matrix. This allows HR advisers and their managers to review current skills against the requirement of the role. This links to quarterly individual reviews and hence to identifying training needs. It is particularly useful for companies such as Capita and Fujitsu where HR skills have to be balanced with commercial skills (to support the running of outsourced contracts) and specific knowledge on TUPE.

IMPLICATIONS

One striking, if soft, piece of evidence from this research is the different perspectives on career paths between the senior staff completing the questionnaire and the junior staff at focus groups. The views of the latter that career moves are more difficult than before supports last year's CIPD research (Tamkin *et al*, 2006) on HR careers and is consistent with a known effect from the segmented nature of the three-legged stool structure. It can be more difficult to progress from administrative roles than before because of the large step-up in expertise or responsibility required.

> 'It is strategic thinking, influencing/political skills and business knowledge that are the most important [in]... business partners.'

The fact that this perception does not appear to have registered with the senior HR managers who completed the survey might be explained by the fact that their preoccupation may be with the professional HR staff found in centres of

expertise and embedded roles. Indeed, there is a sense in which the problems of getting the right sort of people into the business partner roles and getting them to deliver the right sort of contribution seems to dominate their thinking. It is strategic thinking, influencing/political skills and business knowledge that are the most important and challenging. These are quintessentially demands that one would make of business partners. One might think that the skills regarded for other jobs (eg understanding of HR practices and some of the interpersonal skills) are rather taken for granted. However, it is pleasing to note that innovation is now seen to be more of a challenge, as HR will need to be increasingly creative if it is to prosper.

The emphasis in development on formal training rather than on experiential learning, evidenced by the survey, is consistent with the CIPD research on careers (Tamkin *et al*, 2006), although that reported a dearth of development opportunities generally. The case studies showed what can be achieved by testing and developing staff through project working, short-term assignments and absence cover, together with informal learning methods. Similarly, if career blockages are perceived not to exist, then putting in place methods to overcome such barriers will also not register as necessary. The case-study organisations are recognising that if you introduce a shared service centre, then cross-team learning offers benefits in terms of resourcing flexibility and job rotation to give more work variety. However, care must be exercised to ensure that rotation does not lead to ineffective performance (because of unfamiliarity with the work) or irritation to customers who lose established relationships (an identified problem with business partner circulation). Experiential learning through projects, cover and assignments firstly helps build bridges between the different parts of HR and prepares and/or tests whether people can make transitions from one service activity to another. If this is not done, how are the future business partners and experts to be developed? Are they are always to be bought in?

LEARNING POINTS

❖ The leadership of the HR function should look critically at the development needs of the whole function, although action will focus on where there are gaps.

❖ Similarly, the career challenges should be examined for all roles. Construction of a career map may be helpful to see where there are blockages. This should help produce a resourcing plan (balancing internal and external recruitment) and contribute to the above development plan.

❖ Those operating the 'Ulrich' model must be more active in career management to ensure skills development and better internal resourcing options. This means not just support for formal training but engineering development opportunities through short-term assignments, job rotation, project work, absence cover and similar measures.

❖ Knowledge acquisition can be encouraged through formal training/conference attendance, but informal 'lunch and learn'-type sessions can be very helpful.

MANAGING HR TRANSFORMATION   10

❖ **Research respondents are concerned that in structural change there is too much following the ('Ulrich') fashion rather than aligning with business priorities.**

❖ **Too few organisations appear to carry out a base case exercise to establish the 'as is' status before moving to the 'as will be'.**

❖ **The sequence of items of change – structure, process and systems – critically depends on the starting place and the key problem areas.**

❖ **There were many suggestions on how roles ought to be designed so that they are effective and do not overlap.**

INTRODUCTION

This was not a subject explicitly covered in the earlier report, but in that four fifths of our survey respondents had changed their structure in the previous five years, and of those, half had done it in the past 12 months, it appears to be still a hot topic for many organisations.

Our sources for this review are the case-study interviews with those in the throes of HR transformation, or just recovering from it, and the survey, in which we asked what advice respondents would give to those embarking on an HR restructure.

From the survey, the most difficult aspect of change seemed to be defining roles, quickly followed by insufficient resources, skill gaps and ineffective technology. Over a third of respondents gave these answers, and they stood out from the other responses. Most of these issues have been covered earlier (insufficient resources is the exception); here we pick out three other themes that emerged in the research as important.

SETTING OBJECTIVES

Clarity of objectives when setting out on a change programme is one of the messages that emerged from earlier CIPD research (Whittington and Molloy, 2005), but although this was supported by our survey, there were real concerns that organisations are rushing to follow the latest fashion. There are many injunctions to 'ignore management/HR fads', including specifically the 'Ulrich' model.

For example, the advice from one HR manager was: 'Avoid rushing into a "me too" solution because it appears to have worked elsewhere. Each business is different and HR

structures should reflect this.' This suggests that a) HR is not clearly setting out what objectives it is trying to meet by way of change, and b) HR is seeing the challenge through its eyes alone. The risk is that HR's change programme would be disconnected both from the business strategy and any other structural modernisation going on elsewhere. It would thus fail another of the CIPD good change practice tests – that of 'avoiding piecemeal, uncoordinated change initiatives' (Whittington and Molloy, 2005).

The answer is to follow the advice of one of our survey contributors, which is to 'understand the business – ensure that any restructure will add value to the business and will assist with delivering the business strategy.' This means clearly setting out the goals of any change programme and ensuring that they align with business priorities. The Cable and Wireless boxed example below is an illustration of this approach. Nortel's earlier example showed its cost and efficiency targets. The list might seem ambitious to some but it has the benefit of a comprehensive approach that was tackling real deficiencies in the current model. The context of an organisation moving towards a smaller, leaner company provides the logic to focusing on efficiency. Vodafone's business case has similar elements, but there is a strong theme of integration and consistency in a global environment that reflects the international growth of the company.

Cable and Wireless reconstituted its HR philosophy in line with a changed business philosophy. The acquisition of Energis kickstarted changed behaviours that were reflected in HR's transformation. In particular, HR had to be more commercial and performance-oriented. It had to focus on outputs, not inputs, and it had to deliver solutions quickly and fit for purpose. Challenge was seen as legitimate if it drove the business forward.

As part of this first phase of change, organisations should be defining the 'as is' state. It seems that too few organisations carry out such an exercise. Both Nortel and Vodafone undertook activity analysis. This gives an idea not just of the resources involved in HR work but also of how they are deployed in terms of the tasks they execute. This can be extended to a 'stock-take' of functional capability, finding that some staff are high-quality and able to adapt, whereas others are not able to adjust to new ways of working. Other organisations complete a technology review to see how effective they are in meeting HR and customer needs. We have given in the report examples of process mapping – understanding who does what against a whole array of processes. Then there are customer satisfaction statistics and process metrics to be established before any reorganisation to define service levels and how they are perceived.

> '...HR must secure senior management support at the early conceptual phase and sustain it during design and implementation.'

It is also evident from this research and, other CIPD research on technology, devolution and CSR, that HR must secure senior management support at the early conceptual phase and sustain it during design and implementation. Many of the change programmes we have seen – especially structural and technological – have required a business case to be presented, but obtaining management support is more than signing off on the numbers. The executive team may be happy to agree to cost reduction, but are they aware of the implications of working differently? Will executives treat HR differently, or is their view of what HR does stuck in the past? If that does not happen, it can lead to misunderstanding and false expectation down the line. So as one survey correspondent put it: the aim is to 'sell the idea to the board and to make sure they fully understand what the restructuring will be in practice'.

The executive endorsement also then has to be reflected in line manager understanding of, if not full agreement with, the change programme. Once in place, HR has to obtain more than grudging acquiescence in the transformation from managers. Their on-the-ground support for HR is crucial if people management is to prosper, especially if the activity is a shared one.

All this preparatory work can inform the change programme, but it also allows for later evaluation. The number of processes can be cut, activity can be switched away from the

administrative towards strategic work, the resourcing strategy can be determined (especially the need for external recruitment), and organisations can see whether their technology is now more fit for purpose. Those that say that processes are slower or customers are worse-served can be challenged by the evidence.

SEQUENCING THE CHANGE

We have previously seen that different organisations pursued different paths towards transformation. Does one begin with structure and use new teams to reform processes, or vice versa? And where do systems changes come in the cycle: together with process re-engineering, before, or after? The answer depends on the starting point. If there is a dispersed operation, it is almost certainly better to restructure first to mobilise resources to undertake the process re-engineering. Having a new structure in place certainly aids commitment to get processes right, but without knowledge of what improvements can be made, the new structure may be too fat. This suggests progressive tightening of the administrative resource as automation and further process reform is delivered. Cutting staffing too quickly is dangerous if the technology lets an organisation down. A loss of customer confidence could be fatal to the success of the change programme, and personally to its leader – as one interviewee starkly put it. It is better to incur the cost of running two systems in parallel than to cut too soon.

As for the relationship between systems and processes, some argue that organisations need the system to determine how to manage their processes. Critics of this approach would say that this may mean the system tail wags the process dog. In their view, the organisation decides on the processes and then finds the technological solution. Each of these positions is probably right in particular circumstances. Perhaps the most common situation is an iterative interaction between process and system.

> Discussion with the MOD revealed that in their case a review of HR policy principles came first before looking at processes. Having defined these, those responsible for service delivery then had to decide how best to ensure that the processes were delivered to standard. They were also required to ensure that options other than simple e-enablement were available to meet the needs of those roughly 20,000 staff without computer access.

One unintended consequence of HR transformation, as Nortel found, might be that the grade ratio within HR changes and its costs increase. This is because although the numbers within the function might fall, it is the junior staff that are hardest hit. Using data from Saratoga, PriceWaterhouseCoopers (2006) reported that the percentage of managers and professionals as a proportion of HR has increased from 57.3% in 2001 to 63.1% in 2004. There was support for this picture, although less strikingly, in our survey. Numbers in HR had reduced most (in a third of organisations) in the last three years for administrative and junior staff compared with managers and professionals (up in 45%).

There is also the question of time-scale. Royal Mail reported achieving its transformation in six months, but against a background of a burning business platform. Other organisations that have gone for a 'big bang' approach have suffered for it where systems have not worked as expected or there has not been time for the desired culture shift, such as in greater self-reliance by line managers. Where technology has let the function down, it has emphasised the negative aspects of change. In these circumstances, the function did not do enough to promote the savings made. As the CIPD research referred to earlier (Whittington and Molloy, 2005) insists: 'Even where reorganisations are being positively managed, employee [and line manager] support must be continuously worked on.'

> '...change processes often fall down through poor implementation.'

We have seen more gradual approaches. Although this might not be suitable for others, Vodafone's current HR transformation seems to be tight in terms of design (less than six months) but with a long period of implementation (in three years). This is to ensure the buy-in of the global HR community, but it also respects the fact that change processes often fall down through poor implementation. The MOD's HR shared services Agency has also taken three years to construct, but where Vodafone's complexity comes from the international nature of its transformation, the MOD's challenge has been the sheer scale of its dispersed operations.

One survey respondent seemed to take the opposite view: 'Spend about 80% of your time on thinking, listening, exploring ideas, planning and preparation, and 20% on the implementation.' This argument was endorsed by another participant: 'The change programme must be as quick as possible because this can destabilise the most focused team.'

ROLES

A number of the themes that we describe under managing HR transformation apply to roles. Advice we received during this research that might be useful, in light of the number of organisations reporting problems in this area, includes:

❖ Recognise that redesigning roles is a sensitive matter and needs careful handling and good communication, but that it will require tough decisions.

❖ There has to be alignment between the change objectives, how you wish to position the function and the details of individual roles.

❖ In an inclusive manner (involving the HR team and line managers) 'list all HR functions/tasks and then group into roles'. Ensure that HR and senior management requirements match.

❖ Ensure that the purpose, content and deliverables of each role are clear to all. This might include what it is not about, as well as its key elements. The level of detailed description will vary with the job concerned – greater specification for administrative roles, less for business partner.

❖ Identify gaps and overlaps in service provision through role redesign, but also ensure that the recipients of transferred responsibilities understand what they are expected to do. Be certain that 'deleted functions' are indeed unnecessary.

❖ This in particular applies to line managers (because they are less under HR's control (and business partners if they report to business unit heads). Be prepared to 'challenge managers on what their roles are', and do not be too easily deflected by what might be unnecessary in their concerns.

❖ Be prepared to adapt roles in the light of experience.

There is also a specific role design question to be answered that is especially relevant to business partners: what does being strategic look like? It is easy to separate out administrative or clerical work, but not so easy to clarify the difference between operational and strategic. According to Brockbank (1999), operational HR activities refer to the routine day-to-day delivery of basic services, such as administering benefits, assisting in recruitment and arranging basic training, while strategic-level HR activity is more complex and involves the following five criteria:

❖ *long-term* – Is the activity conceptualised to add long-term as opposed to short-term value?

❖ *comprehensive* – Does it cover the entire organisation or isolated components?

❖ *planned* – Is it thought out ahead of time, and is it well documented, or does it occur on an ad hoc basis?

❖ *integrated* – Does it provide a basis for integrating multifaceted activities that might otherwise be fragmented and disconnected?

❖ *high value-added* – Does it focus on issues that are critical for business success, or does it focus on things that must be done but are not critical to financial and market success?

This is a good summary of the characteristics of being strategic. Putting it more simply, to be strategic HR should be involved in issues of long-term importance with high business impact (defined in customers' eyes as much as HR's). Where possible its strategic contribution should be planned and integrated both with the activities of other functions and internally within HR.

CUSTOMER BUY-IN

The CIPD research (Whittington and Molloy, 2005) on change management was very clear that top management and employees had to be proactively engaged. The evidence went further in the case of the former: where political and top management support was absent from the before and after of reorganisation, organisational performance worsened. Those responding with advice on how to effect HR transformation supported these arguments. One participant talked of the need 'to consult business leaders to understand customer needs' and to 'ask employees' as well.

> 'The CIPD research...on change management was very clear that top management and employees had to be proactively engaged.'

If customers are to be bought in, the question this raises is, who are the customers? A long list might include:

❖ the board

❖ senior executives

❖ line managers

❖ employees

❖ ex-employees

❖ shareholders

❖ local communities

❖ suppliers

❖ external business customers.

Having defined the 'who?', the next questions are the 'when?' and the 'what?'. In the case studies we probed an issue that had been identified as problematic before – namely, the extent to which customers were consulted about the new structural model and whether their views were taken into account. At Ernst & Young the changes made to the function were driven by the Executive because they wanted the function to be 'leading-edge'. HR staff told us that they had spoken a lot to customers about changes to their function and emphasised the financial benefits, but it was obvious that managers felt that they were being asked to 'step up to the plate' in relation to the new approach. In particular there was resistance to giving up local HR assistance (especially with respect to resourcing) and the need for reassurance that remote services (like centres of expertise) would do a good job. Emphasis was given to immediate improvements in processes and convincing the line that the centres of expertise would understand their issues.

Vodafone convened a meeting of the HR, Finance and Operations directors to discuss the shape of the new model so that there was high-level customer input in the design. Over a period of two or three years, as its PPPA shared services operation developed, the MOD clarified user requirements. It sought to discover all the people management processes it had to tackle and then grouped them into seven categories. The granular tasks were set out under these headings in some detail. The service delivered then had to meet this specification, which was clearly customer-led.

As one survey correspondent put it, the aim of a consultation exercise is to 'find out what key customers want from the function and get this documented and agreed before restructuring the HR function.' This would help obtain and maintain buy-in. It is also useful if there is subsequent debate about what was agreed and what was not. But there is the challenge highlighted by a survey respondent that the customer is not always right. He/she gave the argument that we would make – namely, 'Ensure that you involve stakeholders at an early stage,' but he/she added the important rider: 'Be prepared to be radical in your thinking and always keep true to the objectives you want to achieve by restructuring – otherwise, you risk ending up with more of the same.'

> 'Be prepared to be radical in your thinking and always keep true to the objectives you want to achieve by restructuring...'

Another correspondent made a similar point: 'Do consult with key customers, but choose an HR operating model which is likely to be the most effective at bringing about the required changes to the structure – not the model which is likely to be the best fit for the organisation in terms of being the most comfortable to implement.'

This point is undoubtedly true, given the recurring theme in this research that managers have not always been keen to accept changes in service provision. This may be because of fears, justified or otherwise, of service deterioration, but also because of a poor understanding of what existing service levels might be – hence the importance of a pre-change status report.

There is also the question of resistance to the changes from within HR. Those within the function are not strictly 'customers', but they are often the most affected by reconfiguration of services and structures. Previous research has shown that HR staff can be the least convinced by change to the function. We heard examples of this in this research.

One senior HR manager commented that their staff had very 'entrenched' views, born of narrow experience that meant that they had not been 'exposed to other thinking'. At another organisation there was apparently huge resistance to the proposed changes to the function, especially from those at senior levels in HR. These managers were giving a negative message to customers about the change programme. This naturally made implementation much more difficult.

These sorts of experiences no doubt underpinned the comments of one survey participant: 'Be prepared for some resistance to role change within the team,' and of another: 'Do not underestimate the difficulty and/or resistance of HR staff to let go of control.' Thus, resistance can come not just from threats to their employment but also from changes to their role or to their relationships to others, such as line managers or employees.

The HR director should play a key role in setting the vision and bringing people along but also in being prepared to adjust to the detail in response to genuine concerns from within the function and legitimate issues from customers. This means active communication and encouragement – 'Motivate, motivate and motivate the HR team. Just because change happens around them does not mean they understand or can deal with it when it affects them,' as a survey correspondent put it.

Another survey respondent summarised the contribution of the HR leader and the job to be done:

Focus on a very clear and strong leader of the function who is able to champion the function at board or other senior level. Ensure the wholesale buy-in of the HR team to changes, and also the HR function's customers/clients/users; it is essential that during the restructuring the customer/clients/users still get what they need from the function. Don't be afraid of change – challenge the existing roles and improve them. Recognise that to deliver service excellence the HR function must understand the business on both tactical and strategic levels.

LEARNING POINTS

❖ Set out the goals of any change programme and ensure that they align with business objectives. The change priorities should deal with real problems, with the existing situation, or address real business (changing) requirements.

❖ Conduct a base case exercise that looks at the resources at HR's disposal, people management skills of line managers, the state of processes and technology, customer views of HR. These data can be used both to identify the need for change and for subsequent evaluation of it.

❖ HR must secure senior management support at the design phase and sustain it during implementation.

❖ Decide on whether to begin with reforming structure before processes and systems on the basis of whether you have the ability to mobilise resources to facilitate process transformation first. If this is not possible, structural change will have to happen first.

❖ Care is required over the design of roles, especially with respect to business partners' strategic input. There should be greater effort made to define what a strategic contribution looks like (see Chapter 6 for more detail).

❖ Define HR's customers and be clear as to their interest in functional performance. Consult them as effectively as you can, but still retain the strategic vision of where the function should be headed (as endorsed by the top team).

❖ Managers will have to put 'real imagination' (Whittington and Molloy, 2005) into finding ways of engaging their customers during the change process. Do not neglect the HR function itself in this process.

APPENDIX 1: SURVEY RESULTS

Set out below is the survey questionnaire with the results of the responses. Percentages are given for the responses to closed questions. These are next to each response option. The number of responses to the question (n) is indicated next to the question. Caution should be taken in interpreting and quoting low figures, because small cell counts lead to unreliable percentages. In general, percentages of 10% or above may be taken to be accurate.

SECTION 1: YOUR ORGANISATION

1   Which sector does your organisation primarily operate in? Please tick one box only:

Manufacturing and production (n=162)

Agriculture and forestry	❑ 1	General manufacturing	❑ 8
Chemicals, oils and pharmaceuticals	❑ 15	Mining and quarrying	❑ 1
Construction	❑ 8	Paper and printing	❑ 4
Electricity, gas and water	❑ 4	Textiles	❑ 1
Engineering, electronics and metals	❑ 28	Other manufacturing/production	❑ 18
Food, drink and tobacco	❑ 12		

Private sector services (n=316)

Professional services (accountancy, advertising, consultancy, legal etc.)	❑ 25	Retail and wholesale	❑ 14
Finance, insurance and real estate	❑ 22	IT services	❑ 6

Hotels, catering and leisure	❏ 3	Communications	❏ 3
Transport, distribution and storage	❏ 9	Call centres	❏ 1
Media (broadcasting and publishing etc)	❏ 5	Other private services	❏ 12

Voluntary, community and not-for-profit (n=64)

Care services	❏ 17	Charity services	❏ 30
Housing association	❏ 38	Other voluntary	❏ 16

Public services (n=278)

Central government	❏ 10	Education	❏ 27
Health	❏ 27	Local government	❏ 26
Other public services	❏ 16		

2 **Will your answers in this survey relate to (please tick one box only)? (n=746)**

❏ 17 an individual business unit?

❏ 10 a corporate centre/head office?

❏ 73 a whole business?

3 **How many people are employed in the unit to which your responses relate?**

. . . .

4 **Is your organisation multinational? (n=772)**

Yes ❏ 36 No ❏ 64

SECTION 2: ABOUT YOUR HR FUNCTION MODEL

5 **How many people are employed in your HR function (please include all whose job is HR, regardless of reporting lines)?**

. . . .

6 **Is the job you are doing best described as (please tick one box only)? (n=784)**

❏ 30 board member?

❏ 58 head of HR function or equivalent?

❏ 8 HR manager?

❏ 2 business partner?

❏ 0   manager of shared service centre?

❏ 3   HR expert?

❏ 2   Other (please specify): . . . .

7 Compared with three years ago, has your HR function in the following categories...

	Grown?	Stayed the same?	Reduced in number?
Senior managers/directors (n=747)	❏ 32	❏ 55	❏ 13
Mid-level management/professionals/ technical specialists (n=732)	❏ 45	❏ 41	❏ 15
Administrators/junior (n=735)	❏ 39	❏ 37	❏ 31

8 Has your HR function changed its structure over the last five years? (n=781)

Yes   ❏ 81   No   ❏ 19   (if no, go to Q.26)

9 When was your HR function restructured? Was it in the last: (n=633)

❏ 53   1 year?

❏ 34   2 to 3 years?

❏ 13   3 to 5 years?

10 Has your HR function been restructured to reflect the so-called Ulrich model (centres of expertise, shared services and business partners)? (n=635)

❏ 29   Yes

❏ 41   No

❏ 28   Partly

❏ 2   Don't know

11 If you have not used the Ulrich model, which structure best describes your model (please tick one box only)? (n=267)

❏ 66   A single HR team with generalists, specialists and administration together

❏ 15   A corporate HR strategy team with operational teams providing all HR services, aligned to business units

❏ 12   A corporate HR strategy team with operational teams providing all HR services, aligned by location

❏ 5   A set of specialist services provided centrally, with business unit HR teams providing the rest of HR services

❏ 2   Other (please specify): . . . .

12 **Was the change driven primarily by (please tick a maximum of three reasons)...(n=632)**

❏ 29   cost reduction?

❏ 34   a need to improve service standards?

❏ 23   a need for more responsive customer service?

❏ 24   repositioning the HR function?

❏ 52   HR becoming a more strategic contributor?

❏ 19   improving the credibility of the function?

❏ 10   line demands for a changed service?

❏ 30   increased business focus?

❏ 24   a need to fit wider organisational change model?

❏ 6   other (please specify): . . . .

13 **Overall, what, if any, have been the main challenges of restructuring HR (please tick a maximum of three)? (n=614)**

❏ 42   Defining roles

❏ 23   Resistance to change in HR

❏ 35   Ineffective technology

❏ 40   Insufficient resources

❏ 3   Inadequate consultancy or supplier support

❏ 38   Dealing with skills gaps

❏ 16   Objections from line-manager customers

❏ 17   Ineffective process change

❏ 13   Recruitment difficulties

❏ 6   Other (please specify): . . . .

14 **Have you introduced centralised provision of shared administrative services (shared services)? (n=631)**

Yes   ❏ 35   No   ❏ 65   (if no, go to Q.19)

15 **If you have introduced centralised provision of shared administrative services (such as a shared service centre), what benefits have you seen (please rate each item on the scale below)? (n=190)**

	No change	Some change	Major change
Cost reduction	❏ 27	❏ 60	❏ 13
Improvement in service quality	❏ 14	❏ 57	❏ 29
More responsive customer service	❏ 21	❏ 49	❏ 30
More commercial approach to HR	❏ 24	❏ 52	❏ 25
Improving the credibility of the function	❏ 25	❏ 45	❏ 31
Repositioning the HR function	❏ 18	❏ 48	❏ 34
HR becoming a more strategic contributor	❏ 19	❏ 50	❏ 31
More satisfied HR staff	❏ 38	❏ 45	❏ 17
HR's time shifted towards more value-adding services	❏ 16	❏ 59	❏ 25

Other (please specify): . . . .

16 **If you have introduced shared services, what problems have you seen (please tick all that apply)? (n=207)**

- ❏ 35 Customer complaints over service
- ❏ 34 Existing HR staff objecting to service centre structure
- ❏ 19 Poor learning within shared services
- ❏ 56 Boundary disputes between parts of HR
- ❏ 41 Gaps in service provision appearing
- ❏ 14 Ineffective escalation procedures
- ❏ 30 Blocks to the development of HR career
- ❏ 36 Communication difficulties within HR
- ❏ 26 Expected savings not achieved
- ❏ 12 None
- ❏ Other (please specify): . . . .

17 Are shared services currently delivered...(n=214)

❏ 69   wholly in-house?

❏ 28   partly outsourced?

❏ 4   wholly outsourced?

18 In three years' time do you expect shared services to be delivered...(n=215)

❏ 42   wholly in-house?

❏ 47   partly outsourced?

❏ 11   wholly outsourced?

19 Have you introduced HR business partners? (n=630)

Yes   ❏ 46   No   ❏ 54   (if no, go to Q.22)

20 What, if any, benefits have you seen in introducing business partners (please tick all that apply)? (n=291)

❏ 76   HR becoming a more strategic contributor

❏ 51   Increased customer satisfaction

❏ 61   Greater line engagement

❏ 53   Repositioning the HR function

❏ 40   Improvement in service quality

❏ 58   Improving the credibility of the function

❏ 69   Increased business focus

❏ 60   People management issues higher on the agenda

❏ 7   Cost reduction

❏ 1   None

❏   Other (please specify): . . . .

21 What, if any, problems have you had with the business partner role (please tick all that apply)? (n=271)

❏ 25   Unclear role

❏ 40   Failure to be strategic

❏ 46   Tension between responding to corporate and business unit needs

❏ 13   Failing to act as service lead for function

❏ 32   Behavioural skill deficiencies

❏ 12   Inadequate knowledge of HR theory and practice

❏ 49   Getting drawn into 'wrong' activities ('going native')

❏ 21   Customer resistance to defined role

❏ 41   Difficulties in finding staff of the right calibre

❏ 18   Coping with demands of employees

❏   Other (please specify): . . . .

22 Have you introduced centres of expertise? (n=630)

Yes   ❏ 36   No   ❏ 64   (if no, go to Q.26)

23 Which subjects have their own centre (please tick all that apply)?

❏ 60   Reward

❏ 67   Recruitment/resourcing

❏ 43   Organisational development

❏ 55   Employee relations/employment law

❏ 36   Talent management/leadership

❏ 32   Health, welfare, well-being

❏ 26   Communications, marketing and PR

❏ 79   Training, learning and development

❏ 30   Management information

❏ 9   Corporate social responsibility

❏   Other (please specify): . . . .

24 What, if any, benefits have you seen from introducing centres of expertise (please tick all that apply)? (n=227)

❏ 69   Deeper professional expertise

❏ 54   Higher-quality advice to HR business partners

❏ 42   Higher-quality advice to executive committee

❏ 51   Greater consistency of advice

❏ 56   HR becomes a more strategic contributor

❏ 38   Repositioning the HR function

❏ 30   More responsive customer service

❏ 47   Better awareness of external good practice

❏ 47   Higher-quality advice to line managers

❏ 3   Improved handling of call centre referrals

❏ 11   Cost reduction

❏ 44   Credibility of the function improved

❏ 36   Improvement in service quality

❏ 0   None

❏ 4   Other (please specify): . . . .

25 **What, if any, problems have you had from introducing centres of expertise (please tick all that apply)? (n=215)**

❏ 12   Over-elaborating services

❏ 16   Advice given to business partners insufficiently tailored to business need

❏ 17   Too much time spent on problems referred to them

❏ 13   Not sufficiently aware of external good practice

❏ 21   Professional skill deficiencies

❏ 28   Poor grasp of business issues

❏ 4   Inappropriate advice given to line managers

❏ 18   Difficulty in developing specialist careers

❏ 30   Recruitment of high-calibre staff

❏ 34   Communication with rest of function

❏ 46   Difficulty in separating out transactional work

❏ 9   None

❏ 7   Other (please specify): . . . .

HR's role and activities

26 **What would you say is the primary role of HR in your organisation?**

. . . .

. . . .

. . . .

27 **What are the main objectives of your HR function (please tick the top five priorities)?** (n=784)

❏ 47   Improve employees' focus on achieving key business goals

❏ 62   Develop employee competencies and capabilities

❏ 16   Cut or control costs

❏ 70   Recruit and retain key staff

❏ 18   Focus employees on customer needs

❏ 39   Secure compliance with employment regulations

❏ 59   Increase employee involvement and engagement

❏ 19   Create a more diverse workforce

❏ 35   Manage major structural change

❏ 61   Improve the way in which people performance is managed

❏ 33   Manage major cultural change

❏ 46   Maximise employee engagement

❏ 3   Change line management behaviour

❏   Other (please specify): . . . .

28 **Please indicate how important you think each of the following is likely to be as a driver of change in people management policies and practices in your organisation in the next three years:** (n=759)

	Very important	Important	Not important
Business strategy/goals	❏ 88	❏ 11	❏ 1
Employee needs	❏ 29	❏ 66	❏ 5
Changes in products or services	❏ 24	❏ 52	❏ 24
Cost pressures	❏ 46	❏ 48	❏ 5
Benchmarking against good HR practice	❏ 22	❏ 62	❏ 15
Culture/values of the organisation	❏ 59	❏ 39	❏ 2
Views of senior management	❏ 55	❏ 44	❏ 1
Line managers	❏ 31	❏ 63	❏ 6
Employment regulation/government policies	❏ 29	❏ 61	❏ 10
Internal customer pressure	❏ 15	❏ 64	❏ 21

	Very important	Important	Not important
HR strategy	❏ 51	❏ 45	❏ 5
Globalisation/competitive pressure	❏ 27	❏ 43	❏ 30

Other (please specify): . . . .

29 How is the time of your HR function divided between (please allocate percentage of time spent between the following three activities)... (n=626)

	3 years ago	Now	3 years' time
administrative activities?	. . . . .50. . .	. . . . .36. . .	. . . . .24. . .
operational HR work?	. . . . .38. . .	. . . . .41. . .	. . . . .41......
strategic input?	. . . . .12. . .	. . . . .23. . .	. . . . .35. . .

30 In terms of the time you spend on the following activities (please indicate by ticking which are the three most time-consuming and which are the three most important to the organisation)... (n=775)

	Most time-consuming	Most important
Business strategy	❏ 14	❏ 58
Implementing HR policies	❏ 38	❏ 16
Developing HR strategy and policy	❏ 28	❏ 64
Providing specialist HR input to wider business issues	❏ 30	❏ 49
Providing support for line managers	❏ 71	❏ 37
Helping employees	❏ 26	❏ 9
Change management	❏ 36	❏ 49
Updating your own HR knowledge	❏ 5	❏ 9
HR administration	❏ 52	❏ 5

31 As well as typical HR activities, does the HR function have responsibility for any of the following? (n=753)

	Lead	Part/joint	No involvement
Organisation design	❏ 22	❏ 67	❏ 11
Facilities management	❏ 12	❏ 22	❏ 66
Internal communications	❏ 24	❏ 63	❏ 13
Health and safety	❏ 35	❏ 42	❏ 22
Corporate social responsibility	❏ 14	❏ 57	❏ 29
Corporate branding	❏ 4	❏ 43	❏ 53

32 Please indicate how responsibility is allocated between the HR function and the line in terms of how decisions are taken in the following areas: (n=768)

	Line	Mainly line	Shared	Mainly HR	HR
Recruitment and selection	❏ 8	❏ 21	❏ 55	❏ 13	❏ 3
Pay and benefits	❏ 2	❏ 5	❏ 28	❏ 45	❏ 20
Employee relations	❏ 0	❏ 6	❏ 40	❏ 39	❏ 15
Training and development	❏ 2	❏ 8	❏ 49	❏ 33	❏ 9
Implementing redundancies	❏ 1	❏ 3	❏ 34	❏ 38	❏ 24
Work organisation	❏ 15	❏ 40	❏ 37	❏ 7	❏ 2

33 Had it been your intention for line managers to take more responsibility for people management than recorded above? (n=774)

Yes ❏ 72   No ❏ 28

34 What has restricted progress? (n=710)

Line manager issues:

	Not at all	A fair amount	A great deal
Skills	❏ 7	❏ 55	❏ 38
Time	❏ 8	❏ 49	❏ 43
Training	❏ 14	❏ 61	❏ 25
Disposition	❏ 19	❏ 51	❏ 30
Priorities	❏ 8	❏ 45	❏ 47

HR issues:

	Not at all	A fair amount	A great deal
Reluctance to let go	❏ 57	❏ 38	❏ 5
Lack of management encouragement to devolve	❏ 35	❏ 51	❏ 15
Lack of role clarity	❏ 41	❏ 48	❏ 11
Restrictive HR processes, policies or structures	❏ 54	❏ 36	❏ 9

Technology issues:

	Not at all	A fair amount	A great deal
Poor manager self-service capability	❏ 22	❏ 41	❏ 37
Poor employee self-service capability	❏ 21	❏ 39	❏ 40

35 How do you assess the performance of HR (please indicate in the table below the methods used to measure particular aspects of HR performance by ticking boxes as appropriate)? (n=737)

	Costs, such as salary costs of the function	Ratios, such as HR staff per head	Outputs, such as courses provided	Outcomes, such as absence rates
The efficiency of the HR function	❏ 50	❏ 48	❏ 33	❏ 49
The effectiveness of the HR function	❏ 23	❏ 23	❏ 39	❏ 56
The quality of service delivered by HR	❏ 11	❏ 11	❏ 38	❏ 46
People management practice	❏ 10	❏ 11	❏ 29	❏ 56
The impact of HR on organisational performance	❏ 24	❏ 14	❏ 26	❏ 55

	Line manager survey/ opinions	Employee surveys	Business performance measures	Customer satisfaction
The efficiency of the HR function	❏ 37	❏ 40	❏ 50	❏ 34
The effectiveness of the HR function	❏ 46	❏ 43	❏ 50	❏ 35
The quality of service delivered by HR	❏ 53	❏ 41	❏ 35	❏ 40
People management practice	❏ 36	❏ 47	❏ 41	❏ 25
The impact of HR on organisational performance	❏ 31	❏ 28	❏ 60	❏ 24

Other (please specify): . . . .

36 How do you think your CEO would score the performance of the HR function for each of the following dimensions (please tick as appropriate)? (n=689)

	Strongly positive	Positive	Neither postive nor negative	Negative	Strongly negative
Contribution to business performance	❏ 21	❏ 59	❏ 17	❏ 3	❏ 0
Closeness to business	❏ 26	❏ 59	❏ 12	❏ 3	❏ 0

	Strongly positive	Positive	Neither postive nor negative	Negative	Strongly negative
Calibre of people in the function	❏ 23	❏ 55	❏ 17	❏ 4	❏ 1
Influence on board decisions	❏ 21	❏ 50	❏ 24	❏ 5	❏ 0
Relationship with the line	❏ 26	❏ 60	❏ 13	❏ 2	❏ 0
Quality of HR processes	❏ 12	❏ 49	❏ 27	❏ 11	❏ 1
Ability to offer an independent perspective	❏ 34	❏ 55	❏ 9	❏ 2	❏ 0

37 On each of the following key dimensions, please indicate (1) where the HR function in your organisation is now, and (2) where you believe it will need to be in future: (n=765)

(1) Where your organisation is **now**

	1	2	3	4	5	
Strategic	❏ 3	❏ 16	❏ 44	❏ 32	❏ 5	Operational
Proactive	❏ 5	❏ 24	❏ 35	❏ 31	❏ 5	Reactive
Tailored practice	❏ 8	❏ 42	❏ 38	❏ 10	❏ 1	Off-the-shelf
Business-driven	❏ 10	❏ 40	❏ 36	❏ 13	❏ 2	Employee-driven
Specialist	❏ 2	❏ 13	❏ 42	❏ 30	❏ 13	Generalist

(2) Where you believe your organisation needs to be **in future**

	1	2	3	4	5	
Strategic	❏ 28	❏ 53	❏ 15	❏ 4	❏ 1	Operational
Proactive	❏ 38	❏ 54	❏ 6	❏ 1	❏ 1	Reactive
Tailored practice	❏ 22	❏ 50	❏ 22	❏ 5	❏ 1	Off-the-shelf
Business-driven	❏ 33	❏ 47	❏ 17	❏ 3	❏ 0	Employee-driven
Specialist	❏ 9	❏ 30	❏ 45	❏ 10	❏ 6	Generalist

SECTION 3: HR SKILLS AND CAREERS

38 Please indicate which three of the following list of competencies/capabilities you believe are (1) most important to establishing the function's effectiveness and credibility in the organisation, and (2) its biggest challenge in terms of acquiring or developing these skills: (n=767)

	(1) Most important	(2) Biggest challenge
Influencing/political skills	❏ 51	❏ 58
Understanding of HR practices	❏ 27	❏ 8
Empathy/communication/listening skills	❏ 16	❏ 8
Leadership ability	❏ 34	❏ 34
Strategic thinking	❏ 54	❏ 53
Ability to deliver against targets	❏ 40	❏ 29
Business knowledge	❏ 45	❏ 38
Negotiating skills	❏ 8	❏ 11
Integrity	❏ 23	❏ 4
Willingness to innovate	❏ 17	❏ 34

39 How are you closing any gaps in skills (please tick all that apply)? (n=763)

❏ 57 CIPD study

❏ 52 Internal HR courses/seminars

❏ 72 External courses

❏ 12 Temporary cover (internal)

❏ 36 Project-working in other areas

❏ 36 Recruitment

❏ 13 External degree-level study

❏ 52 External conferences

❏ 13 Temporary cover (external)

❏ 24 Short-term assignments

❏ 10 Other (please specify): . . . .

40 How have the changes to the way HR is organised influenced careers within HR (please tick all that apply)? (n=710)

❏ 17   Made it more difficult to develop people

❏ 65   Created more opportunity

❏ 31   Made it easier to move between different HR roles

❏ 19   Made it more difficult to develop people into new roles

❏ 17   Made it more difficult to enter the function

❏ 21   Made mid-career moves into HR easier

❏ 22   Made HR careers more siloed

❏ 4   Other (please specify): . . . .

41 What advice would you give to anyone about to restructure their HR function?

. . . .

. . . .

. . . .

. . . .

APPENDIX 2: CASE-STUDY SUMMARIES

VODAFONE

Vodafone is the world's leading international mobile telecommunications group with equity interests in 27 countries across five continents. It is a young company: the UK's first mobile call was made as recently as January 1985. It has eight offices in the UK besides its Newbury headquarters. It employs around 11,000 people in the UK and about 66,000 worldwide.

Its HR function employs about 160 in the UK. Over the next three years, the company is engaged in an HR transformation project looking at structures, processes and relationships with line management and customers. The HR structure is organised as follows.

❖ Business partners are the primary HR interface with the business leadership community, responsible for defining and executing local people plans and driving the transformational people agenda.

❖ Local HR managers, in highly regulated markets, are involved in interpretation of policy, especially employee relations issues and advice to line managers as well as employees.

❖ An advisory call centre, in the UK, is used by employees, line managers and leaders for guidance on policy, employee relations, process and administrative support.

❖ A global shared service centre is currently being developed in Hungary.

❖ Centres of expertise at different levels:

❖ global (global policy design, development of standard processes, principles and strategy)

❖ regional (guidance on implementation)

❖ local (actual delivery of standard processes; design/ implementation of local policies/non-standard processes, local employee relations).

Managers and employees will have access to self-service common technology at the end of the HR Transformation programme.

In the Vodafone model the line manager is becoming increasingly accountable for the company's People Strategy and employees' experience at work.

NORTEL

Nortel is a recognised leader in technology and information companies. These cover networks, multimedia and applications. Its aims are to speed processes and improve networks, connecting people with information. It employs about 5,200 people in the UK and 30,000 worldwide, where it operates in a 150 different countries. Its HR function employs approximately 95 people in the UK.

Nortel undertook an HR Evolution Project. This comprises implementing SAP self-service worldwide, process standardisation and cost reduction within HR to fit the reshaped business. The self-service project was delivered in 16 months. HR is organised as follows.

❖ Business partners support individual business units.

❖ There are four shared service centres across the world (for the Americas, for EMEA, France and Hong Kong covering Asia/Pacific), each comprising a call centre and transaction processing.

❖ Payroll is executed locally.

❖ There are no centres of expertise, rather four 'core HR strategy' units (employee relations, compensation and benefits, talent and diversity) that look forward and externally and provide governance function. Their new strategies are implemented by the HR Delivery teams.

❖ Six Delivery teams, also in functional units, are the global process designers/owners and are the port of call for manager/employee complex queries referred by the shared service centre. They also handle change requests that sit outside standard policy.

SURREY COUNTY COUNCIL

The Council employs over 33,000 people and provides a full range of services for local citizens. Of its £1.4 billion expenditure nearly half is payroll cost.

Prior to reorganisation, HR employed 400 staff. Five heads of HR represented the various departments. Now HR has a Head of HR and OD and 40 staff and is organised as follows:

❖ two outsourced services – The first supports an employee base of 20,000 and is outsourced to a third-party provider except for payroll, and pensions. The other is insourced, undertaken within a Corporate Services shared service centre, together with IT, Procurement and Finance

❖ an information bureau staffed by non-HR people – They are expected to handle 80% of all enquiries including telephone, fax and email. This may include in many cases referring people back to the County Council's self-service intranet site

❖ a duty desk (acting as the second level up in call centre escalation), a case-work section (that deals with the calls not dealt with by the duty desk) and a project team

❖ business partners for each department

❖ a policy unit (covering reward/recognition and employee relations), a separate learning and development design unit (with outsourced delivery)

❖ a strategy team (covering organisational development, workforce planning and career succession planning).

Future development of the HR function will include a review of the outsourcing approach with consideration of further outsourcing or insourcing. Greater investment in HR has been agreed to lead the county in organisational design for 'a twenty-first-century Council'.

CAPITA

Capita is the leading UK business process outsourcing and professional services company and delivers a variety of outsourced customer and administrative services to public and private sector clients. These include HR services that cover the complete employee lifecycle (eg for the BBC) and activities as diverse as collecting London congestion charges to Corporate Health Solutions. Capita now employs 27,800 people.

HR is structured as follows.

❖ Forty-four business partners support directors and managers of the variety of businesses across Capita, and a small specialist team delivers HR strategy, policy, employee relations and reward. Business partners are expected to develop enough functional expertise to support line management, but the latter has wide discretion in people management terms.

❖ An insourced shared service centre handles HR transactional work for their in-house customers.

❖ Centres of excellence deliver occupational health, pensions, recruitment, learning and development and outplacement services.

The company makes extensive use of manager and employee self-service.

HAMPSHIRE COUNTY COUNCIL

Hampshire County Council is a four-star local authority and one of the largest in the country. It currently serves a population of 1.26 million and employs more than 30,000 staff. The Council provides a full range of services for the people of Hampshire including environment, recreation and heritage, property, business and regulatory, and children and adult services.

Prior to the new structure, HR was organised as individual personnel teams per department, reporting to the head of HR, with a central policy unit. Now it has:

❖ business partners for each of the six main departments

❖ a centre of excellence looking specifically at resourcing, employment practice and occupational health, but also including an employment support line

❖ a shared payroll operation, but no shared service centre as such.

The centre of expertise currently picks up the administrative work.

Over the next five years the likelihood is that HR will be smaller and become more integrated with other parts of the organisation, including IT and Finance. It may adopt more of a cross-functional consultancy/OD model. The expectation is that a cross-functional shared service centre will be created linked to the contact centre. HR consultants will be in the centre of excellence.

HER MAJESTY'S REVENUE AND CUSTOMS

HM Revenue and Customs (HMRC) was formed in April 2005 from the merger of Inland Revenue and HM Customs and Excise Departments. HMRC is responsible for collecting the bulk of tax revenue, as well as paying tax credits and child benefits, and strengthening the UK's frontiers. It employs 94,000 employees.

It reorganised its HR function in Spring 2007. A temporary structure was created when the Inland Revenue and Customs and Excise merged. A more radical change to HR was considered, but it was decided to look at it again once the priorities of talent management and workforce change had been addressed.

The newly unveiled HR structure comprises:

❖ a corporate 'service delivery' unit, made up of HR services, a service improvement team, learning delivery and specialist delivery teams, including case management, pay casework and business people support (a kind of modern welfare function)

❖ a strategy and consultancy group (including strategy on skills/development, reward and employee relations/culture)

❖ business partners together with learning and development advisers embedded in business units reporting to the head of Business Partnering who is part of the strategy and consultancy group

❖ performance and planning – an internal finance and measurement team

❖ a separate leadership and talent division, created to give emphasis to talent management and development

❖ a temporary team called 'workforce change' responsible for effectively managing the downsizing of HMRC.

ERNST & YOUNG

Ernst & Young is an equity partnership with 420 partners who own the business. Salaried employees work for the firm. The partnership elects a chair who appoints a board overseen by a council. It is a very democratic organisation.

The first HR partner was appointed in 1999, when the executive decided that it wanted a fully professional HR function. An 'Ulrich'-style restructure was introduced in 2000.

At present HR has:

❖ four HR teams, led by business partners, in each of the three business units, and in support services

❖ a support unit/shared service centre

❖ a policy and strategy unit. This is divided into:

    ❖ employee relations/reward (including pensions)

    ❖ strategic resourcing (HR planning, women returnees, graduates)

    ❖ learning and development (partner development, leadership)

    ❖ people marketing.

FIREFLY COMMUNICATIONS

Firefly is a small PR company working with large and small organisations alike within the consumer technology, business technology, consumer brand, business-to-business, professional services, not-for-profit and public sectors. It has been established 18 years. It has 45 people in the London office, a further five in Scotland, and also small satellite offices in Paris, Munich and Stockholm.

The HR manager is the only dedicated HR person. The CEO acts as the HR director and is focused on the people side of the business. The director's PA helps on administrative work.

The HR manager develops the HR strategy and looks after recruitment and retention; compensation and benefits; training and development; employment law; policy and procedures; internal communication and counselling. She is responsible for all aspects from administration to strategy. She works closely with the board (including non-executives), the operational board (which consists of the CEO, the MD, head of Consumer, head of Corporate and Finance).

Strategy is decided at board level, day-to-day running by the management team which is formed by the account directors and the HR manager.

REFERENCES

BECKER, B. and HUSELID, M. (1999)

'Overview: strategic human resource management in five leading firms', *Human Resource Management*, Vol. 38, 287–301

BOUDREAU, J. and RAMSTAD, P. (2003)

'Strategic HRM measurement in the 21st century: from justifying HR to strategic talent leadership', in Goldsmith, M., Gandossy, R. and Efron, M. (eds) *HRM in the 21st Century*. Chichester, John Wiley & Sons

BROCKBANK. W. (1999)

'If HR were really strategically proactive: present and future directions in HR's contribution to competitive advantage', *Human Resource Management*, Vol. 38 (4), 337–52

CABRERA, A. and CABRERA, E. F. (2003)

'Strategic human resource evaluation', *HR Planning Society*, Vol. 26, March

CIPD (2003)

HR Survey: Where we are, where we are heading. Survey report. London, Chartered Institute of Personnel and Development

CIPD (2006a)

The Changing HR Function: The key questions. London, Chartered Institute of Personnel and Development

CIPD (2006b)

Offshoring and the Role of HR. Survey report. London, Chartered Institute of Personnel and Development

CIPD (2006c)

2006 Reward Management Survey. London, Chartered Institute of Personnel and Development

CIPD (2006d)

Risk and Performance: HR's role in managing risk. London, Chartered Institute of Personnel and Development

CIPD (2007)

The Changing HR Function. Survey report. London, Chartered Institute of Personnel and Development

CUNNINGHAM, I. and HYMAN, J. (1999)

'Devolving human resource responsibilities to the line', *Personnel Review*, Vol. 28, No. 1–2

DELOITTE CONSULTING (2005)

Global HR Transformation. Survey report

HIRSH, W., CARTER, A., STREBLER, M. and BALDWIN, S. (2008)

Customer Views of HR. Brighton, Institute for Employment Studies

HUSELID, M. A. (1995)

'The impact of human resource management practices on turnover, productivity and corporate financial performance', *Academy of Management Journal*, Vol. 38, 635–72

HUTCHINSON, S. and PURCELL, J. (2007)

Learning and the Lne: The role of line managers in training, learning and development. London, Chartered Institute of Personnel and Development

IRS (2006)

'Roles and responsibilities 2006: benchmarking the HR function', *Employment Review 839*, 20 January, 9–17

LAWLER, E., BOUDREAU, J. W. and MOHRMAN, S. (2006)

Achieving Strategic Excellence. Palo Alto, CA: Stanford University Press

LEGGE, K. (1989)

'Human resource management: a critical analysis', in Storey, J. *New Perspectives on Human Resource Management*. London, Routledge

MCGOVERN, P., GRATTON, L., HOPE-HAILEY, V., STILES, P. and TRUSS, C. (1997)

'Human resource management on the line?', *Human Resource Management Journal*, Vol. 7, No. 4

PARRY, E., TYSON, S., SELBIE, D. and LEIGHTON, R. (2007)

HR and Technology: Impact and advantages. London, Chartered Institute of Personnel and Development

PERSONNEL TODAY (2006)

'Getting HR strategy in tune with business goals', *Personnel Today.* 16 May

PORTER, M. E. (1985)

Competitive Advantage: Creating and sustaining superior performance. New York, Free Press

PRICEWATERHOUSECOOPERS (2006)

Key Trends in Human Capital: A Global Perspective

PURCELL, J. and HUTCHINSON, S. (2007)

Rewarding Work: The vital role of line managers. London, Chartered Institute of Personnel and Development

PURCELL, J., KINNIE, N., HUTCHINSON, S., RAYTON, B. and SWART, J. (2003)

Understanding the People and Performance Link: Unlocking the black box. London, Chartered Institute of Personnel and Development

REDDINGTON, I. (2005)

Making CSR Happen: The contribution of people management. London, Chartered Institute of Personnel and Development

REILLY, P. and WILLIAMS, T. (2006)

Strategic HR: Building the capability to deliver. London, Gower

STOREY, J. (1992)

Developments in the Management of Human Resources. Oxford, Blackwell

TAMKIN, P. (2005)

The Contribution of Skills to Business Performance. London, DfES

TAMKIN, P., REILLY, P. and HIRSH, W. (2006)

Managing HR Careers: Emerging trends and issues. London, Chartered Institute of Personnel and Development

TORRINGTON, D. (1998)

'Crisis and opportunity in HRM: the challenge for the personnel function', in Sparrow, P. and Marchington, M. (eds) *Human Resource Management: The new agenda.* London, Pitman/Financial Times

TYSON, S. and FELL, A. (1986)

Evaluating the Personnel Function. London, Hutchinson

ULRICH, D. (1997)

Human Resource Champions: The next agenda for adding value and delivering results. Boston, MA: Harvard Business Press

ULRICH, D. and BROCKBANK, W. (2005)

The HR Value Proposition. Boston, MA: Harvard Press

ULRICH, D., YOUNGER, J. and BROCKBANK, W. (FORTHCOMING)

The Next Evolution in HR Organization: working paper

WHITTAKER, S. and MARCHINGTON, M. (2003)

'Devolving HR responsibility: threat, opportunity or partnership', *Employee Relations,* Vol. 25, No. 3

WHITTINGTON, R. and MOLLOY, E. (2005)

HR's Role in Organising: Shaping change. Research report. London, Chartered Institute of Personnel and Development